Rewired Restored

Healing the Nervous System in a Dopamine Addicted World

Tony Crandall

ISBN: 979-8-9954755-0-7

Contents

Thank you for trying to protect me.
But I am safe now.
This is my new life.

Chapter One

PURPLE RAIN

It was Day 53 of my recovery, and I had just dropped off my younger son for his junior winds concert at Capital University. He's a high school freshman, but he carries himself with that quiet seriousness musicians have. Helping him wheel his tuba into the hall, watching him disappear into the practice rooms with the other players — something in me felt steady, proud, grounded. Not the old manic pride, not the performative "look at my kid" pride. Just a simple, solid father standing in the right place at the right time.

I had an hour to burn before the concert started, so I grabbed lunch at Brassica and a Starbucks next door, then headed back to my car. Reclining into the leather seat of the German machine a former version of myself thought he needed, I queued up my Spotify playlist and let myself exhale.

It was a perfect Ohio autumn afternoon. The sun filtered through yellow, red, and orange leaves in a way only fall light can manage — warm, slanted, almost holy. The sky was a deep cobalt, the kind that only exists for a few weeks each year before winter flattens everything out.

A few tracks in, "Purple Rain" came on.

I've listened to that song for forty-one years. I've used it as fuel, background noise, or emotional wallpaper. But on that day — sitting on Capital's campus, caffeine in my hand, forty-plus years of chaos behind me — the song didn't wash over me. It cut straight through me.

For the first time, I actually thought about the words.

Why purple rain?

Purple rain isn't a color. It's a collision.

It's the moment when deep love and deep sorrow meet and create something that can heal.

It's the wish that both people's pain — yours and theirs — could be washed away.

That wish only comes from someone who genuinely loved and respected not just the other person, but themselves too.

The tears hit instantly. No warning. No drama. Just truth breaking through the drywall of my old mind.

Redemption?

Resurrection?

No. Those weren't the words.

The only word big enough for what I felt was **gratitude**.

Gratitude that I even *wanted* to understand the song... that I finally *could*...that whatever had been frozen and numb in me for decades was thawing exactly where I sat.

Layers of consciousness that had been sealed shut for fifty-eight years were waking up. I felt alive. I felt present. I felt whole — not manic, not euphoric, not chemically spiked — just whole.

Fifty-eight years of chaos and coping in the extremes.

And now, a glimpse of what life can be when your brain finally stops lying to you.

The tears kept coming, but they felt clean.

I am healing.

And my life will never be the same.

Chapter Two

THE ARCHITECTURE OF SURVIVAL

The Childhood Foundation

My earliest memories don't contain warmth. No laughter. No security. Just a sense of *being alone* in a world where no one was coming.

The very first one: I'm on the concrete patio of a rented house near Marion, Ohio. I'm two years old, blowing bubbles. The plastic bottle tips over and spills across the concrete, making everything slick. Right then I have to go to the bathroom. I run to the so-called training toilet in the bathroom... and I don't make it. That's it — my earliest memory. **Failure. Shame.** That early, my nervous system was already wiring itself around guilt.

Another time, in that same house, I climbed on top of a dresser near my crib so I could see out the window. I got stuck. I called for help. Then I yelled. Then I screamed. Nobody came. Nobody even checked. So I figured it out myself — pulled open the drawers, stepped down one level at a time, and freed myself.

It's hard to overstate how formative it is to scream for help as a child and have the universe answer back with silence. Over time you stop expecting rescue. You become your own solution.

Not long after that, my mother had friends over. They were sitting in the sunken living room talking. I crawled behind the couch, then into the foyer, and opened one of those late-60s snack trays — the ones that fold up and collapse. I tried to climb onto it to get someone's attention. It buckled under me and I smashed face-first into the slate. It was loud. Violent. Three feet from the adults. Nobody turned around. I didn't cry. I just disappeared back into the shadows.

That's what happens when a child learns he's invisible.

Then came the first real humiliation. My brother and I asked my dad what motor oil did. He told us it "cleaned and protected," so we grabbed the can and squeezed it everywhere — across the garage walls and floor. When he saw it, he found the thinnest belt he owned and made us pull our pants down. Seven hard stripes (his literal understanding of the Bible you see), bare skin. I remember thinking the pain wasn't the real wound — the confusion was. I didn't know what rule I had broken. I just knew punishment arrived with no explanation.

While my dad was building our next house, the basement was just a giant pit in the ground. That's where the older neighborhood kids introduced themselves. They grabbed me by the arms, dragged me to the edge of the hole, and threatened to throw me in. I was three. That was my welcome to the neighborhood.

To the west lived "Caveman Jim," a walking stereotype of rural chaos — porn mags stacked everywhere, a rabbit farm, poached deer hanging from trees, and a household run with intimidation. His boys were wild and unsupervised. One of my first recollections of them was the oldest kid chasing the middle kid out of the house... oldest kid threw a dart and hit his brother in the back of the head... the dart stuck!!! Holy shit lol!! That's where I first saw pornography at five years old. And where I first chewed tobacco and smoked a cheap cigar at the same time, making myself violently sick — the kind of sickness you don't forget.

Across the road was the concrete block salesman whose son threatened to cut me into pieces "like those butter-rum Lifesavers you're eating" with an open pocket knife he held in front of me. His sister, chain-smoking in a tube top at age 12, always had matches for me to play with. There was no such thing as a safe adult. No one in that world was watching out for anyone.

Once, a sheriff's cruiser stopped in the middle of the road while I was riding my bike. Lights flashing. Siren off. I asked if I was "under arrest." I didn't know what else to say. He followed me home and spoke to my parents. Nothing happened after that — no conversation, no comfort, no explanation. Just more silence.

I was raised Christian Scientist. No doctors. No medicine. Pain was something you endured, ignored, or prayed through. The only time we went to a professional was the dentist — and several times, at my request, he didn't use novocaine... you see Christian Scientists didn't take medicine. I had cavities constantly because my diet was trash, so I sat through countless fillings, white-knuckled and grinding through the pain. I learned early that suffering was something you don't talk about.

I was underweight and a bully magnet. One kid turned his class ring around and cracked me on the skull with it on the bus. My older brother watched. Did nothing. That pretty much sums up the support I got from the home team.

The only comfort I had was sucking my thumb — until someone saw me do it in public and humiliated me. I stopped that day. My dogs were the real family: Ginger, my Irish Setter, and later Nicholas, my German Shepherd. They were safe. Predictable. Loyal. Everything humans weren't. My warmth. My heart.

Boundaries didn't exist in my house. Once, I made a corncob pipe, stuffed it with whatever I could find, and smoked it. When I came into the house my mom walked straight up to me, reached into my jacket pocket, and pulled it out — like she had been watching me the whole time. It wasn't discipline; it was intrusion. It was years later that I learned exactly why this hit so hard.

Another time, when I was around seven, I built a fuel–air bomb from a milk jug. It ignited faster than I expected and blew half my hair, eyebrows, and eyelashes off. My brother called my mom at work. She expected to come home to a corpse.

The worst was the scarlet fever. I visited my brother at college for Little Sibs Weekend and came home sick. My temperature hit 105.7 as measured by the health department workers my mother called to document a "communicable disease." I hallucinated that the house was a chessboard. My skin blistered and peeled off my hands and feet. I recovered alone for two weeks — no school, no doctors, no medicine. By the time I returned, the gym teacher forced me to wrestle another kid during class. I was weak, dizzy, but I still held my own. That was childhood: survive, don't complain, and keep moving.

I played sports in middle and high school because I thought I had to for some reason. I mostly hoped that no one noticed how skinny or unskilled I was. Academically, I did the bare minimum and spent most of my energy vandalizing things with friends or partying. Eventually I became enough of a discipline problem that I decided to graduate early. That summer, I worked during the day to pay for tutoring in government and English so I could enter The Ohio State University.

My first year was a disaster — a 17-year-old with no life skills, no structure, no guidance. I used freshman forgiveness on nearly every class and salvaged a 1.0 GPA. I thought I wanted to be an engineer like my dad but didn't have the discipline or internal stability to make that real.

One day I'm in Independence Hall, standing at a urinal after an exam. There's graffiti on the wall: "The limit of your engineering GPA as it approaches zero = business." It hit me like divine intervention. My uncle Larry was an accountant — that was my new direction. For the first time in my life, there was a *path.*

I worked hard. I aced nearly every course in a very difficult major, but my GPA still wasn't Big Four-worthy. I interned at a national specialty foods manufacturer where the CFO set up a lunch with our Big Four auditor. The guy looked across the table and told me, flatly, I wasn't good enough to join them. Not "your grades." *You.*

It branded me.

But it also lit a fuse.

I graduated into a recession. The place that I interned eventually hired me full-time as a staff accountant under a controlling, context-free boss who treated work like a punishment. I carried half the load: journal entries, pricing, inventory valuation, tax schedules, fixed assets — the whole thing. I knew so much more than the auditors who looked down on me. One day, a sales guy told me I was on "a one-way career path to lower middle-level management." That was it.

I killed the GMAT. I applied to one business school — Case Western — with a single goal: become a consultant at a Big Four consulting firm.

Determination had become direction.

And direction became salvation. I was the first in my graduating class to receive an offer.

The Overachiever Identity

I didn't wake up one morning and decide to become an overachiever.

It wasn't ambition.

It wasn't hunger for success.

It wasn't some inner competitive drive.

It was survival long before it ever looked like achievement.

I grew up in a home where emotions were either denied or spiritualized away, where discipline replaced connection, where shame lived under the floorboards, and where I never truly felt "seen." No one mirrored me. No one guided me. No one told me who I was or what I could become. My nervous system learned early that worthiness wasn't something I had — it was something I had to earn.

So when I reached further into the 1980s and landed at Principia College — after nearly failing out of Ohio State — I walked into my first clean slate. A reset. A chance to reinvent myself without the weight of my past following me. And at that exact moment, the right person appeared.

Brilliant. Charismatic. Sharp as a razor and just as precise. He had been my brother's professor years earlier, but when I stepped into his classroom, I felt something I had never felt before: admiration. I wanted his respect. I wanted to measure up to a man like that. This wasn't academic motivation — this was emotional ignition.

I'd gotten a D in introductory accounting at Ohio State. But for this professor?

I sat in the front row.

I leaned in.

I participated.

I worked until every problem was solved flawlessly. Elegantly.

I became the best student in the class.

It wasn't about the subject.

It wasn't about accounting.

It was about something much deeper.

Excellence brought belonging.

Performance brought validation.

Being impressive made me feel safe.

And I didn't know it then, but that moment was the birth of the Overachiever Identity — the first time achievement became a shield over the wounds of being unseen.

After Principia, the pattern repeated.

I met the CFO — and later the president — of the national specialty foods manufacturer. Tall. Impeccably dressed. Sharp. Confident. A man with executive presence long before I even had language for it. He liked me. Respected me. Saw something in me. And instantly, the same instinct lit up inside me:

Make him proud.

Meet his standard.

Rise to the level of the man I admired.

That's what people never understand about overachievers:

We don't chase success.

We chase the people who awaken our potential.

And we are loyal to them forever.

At that time every finance and accounting process at that company was paper-based — fixed assets tracked manually, processes scattered, chaotic, inefficient. I saw ambiguity and wanted to bring order to it. So, I coded a fixed asset system in dBase 4+, a rudimentary database at the time. I streamlined the process, added controls, automated tasks, and created something that actually worked.

I did it for the organization, yes.

But if I'm telling the truth...

I did it for the CFO.

I wanted him to see I could think.

I wanted him to see I could solve problems before they were handed to me.

I wanted to live up to the man he was.

He was a pivotal figure in my early career — and I still think of him with respect and gratitude.

Later, when I left for Case Western, I nervously asked him to be my mentor. I don't know if he remembers me today, but I remember him — not as a boss, but as one of the men whose presence shaped me.

Meeting and working with these people were not mistakes.

They weren't delusions.

They weren't projections.

They were archetypes — the men I looked to when I didn't have a father who could guide me emotionally. They represented a future version of myself. They called something forward in me.

And the childhood version of me — unseen, unmirrored, uncertain — ran toward that with everything he had.

That's how it begins.

Overachievement starts as protection.

It becomes identity.

And before long, it becomes the only way you know how to feel safe in the world.

This is how the Big Four later found me — a young man already conditioned to read expectations, exceed them, win approval, and treat performance like oxygen.

What I didn't know then was that the same identity that built my career would later burn me to the ground.

But in those early days, it felt like becoming someone new.

Someone important.

Someone worthy.

Someone finally seen.

Consulting as Identity

If the overachiever identity was born in the quiet rows of Principia College, then consulting was where it grew teeth. Consulting didn't just become my career — it became the identity I wore like armor. And I know exactly why.

I didn't grow up poor, but I grew up watching my father fumble through life. No promotions. No upward trajectory. No confidence. I watched him at fast-food counters, pulling bills from his wallet like he wasn't sure what anything was worth. My mother never let him forget it. I decided early — maybe subconsciously — that would never be me. I wasn't going to live small. I wasn't going to be overlooked. I wasn't going to stay stuck.

And in the mid 90's, nothing symbolized escape from smallness like big consulting.

Consultants had prestige.

Consultants wore sharp suits.

Consultants flew on planes, stayed in hotels, and were trusted with big, messy problems at massive companies.

Consultants were somebody.

That's what drew me — prestige, money, and the identity that came with both.

The name of the global professional services firm I most wanted to join sounded like an empire.

A brand made of polished wood, leather briefcases, and men who walked fast.

I wanted that world.

In the fall of my second year at Case Western, I interviewed on campus with their consulting team. Then I was pulled into a second interview — this one with two partners, at the BP building in downtown Cleveland. The 27th floor. Mahogany walls. The spiral staircase. The receptionist answering the phone with the kind of confidence my childhood never allowed me to imagine.

The morning of the interview, I was sick as hell — fever, sore throat — but there was no chance I was missing this. I'd crawled my way out of failure and invisibility, and destiny was knocking with a mahogany fist.

That's where I met the senior partner.

Brilliant.

Sharp.

Cost-management royalty.

He stood at a tall desk by a window overlooking Lake Erie and Cleveland Stadium, reading the Wall Street Journal like he was born doing it. He asked why I wanted to join the firm, and I didn't give him a cliché answer. I told him the truth:

"I want to be a partner."

A week later, there was a knock at the door of my apartment.

A FedEx box.

Inside was the offer letter — embossed on heavy cotton stationery with the firm insignia. And out spilled a thick, high-quality sweatshirt that said, as loudly as the logo could scream:

"You belong here now."

And God, did that feel good.

The day I started, a window washer fell off his platform near the 30th floor to the parking deck below. Many people in the office saw it and were offered grief counseling.

My first trip was with the senior partner to a technology company headquartered in rural Wisconsin — a town where there are more bars than people. After a long session with the client trying to decode their ERP landscape, we hit one of those bars where they lock the doors and the alcohol is free until someone leaves or uses the bathroom. Neither happened for a while. We got annihilated. And the next morning, we showed up for a full day of interviews and working sessions still half-drunk, still half-invincible.

I didn't understand in any depth what was going on, but that didn't matter. I organized my notes. And I felt like I was part of something big.

From there, I went to a massive Oracle financials and logistics implementation. Hundreds of consultants. No one knew what was happening. It was chaos in a suit. I ended up becoming the cost-accounting lead without actually doing anything meaningful to earn it. I even told the partner about it — and he looked at me and said two things I'll never forget:

"Perception is reality."

"They're spending so much money on us there's no room for anybody else."

Those two lines became part of my consulting DNA.

But the work was grinding me down — a vending-machine room the size of a prison cell, a freezing house trailer in a parking lot of a mozzarella factory in what you could call a small town, population seven. Hairnets in the warehouse, folding chairs, forklift drivers strafing our work area, long days, zero heating, zero connection to anything human or alive.

After a year and a half, I asked to leave.

I threw myself an elaborate rolling off dinner at Jimmy's Dell Bar with my closest friends. The next night in Madison, a manager from St. Louis took me out for drinks on campus and picked up the tab for a bar full of coeds and us. A sly grin spread across his face as he was handed a $4,000 check before he tallied the tip. When the Midwest Express flight crew offered champagne on the flight to Columbus the next morning, I reached for the air sickness bag and prayed that the plane would crash.

And then I landed on the job that changed my life.

Global Automotive Manufacturer #1.

I was a senior consultant then. The client had implemented an ERP system themselves, and it was a disaster. They were in a perpetual month-end close — they couldn't close the books before the next month started. Burnout. Turnover. Chaos.

Enter another defining person in my life.

He was the guy who took young talent and threw them into the deep end. He trusted me before I even trusted myself. But I had a flaw: I over-analyzed things. I thought too long before acting. And in his direct, no-bullshit way, hit me with a line that changed the trajectory of my career:

"Tony, I have every respect in the world for your analytical ability — but I need to get results for this client."

It landed like a nuclear detonation.

I could not fail.

So I didn't.

I built a methodology from scratch.

I pushed myself harder than I ever had.

I took three staff that the client paid for and turned them into a strike team.

And within five months, we brought the client's close cycle from 30+ days down to six.

The operation stabilized.

People could go home again.

There was no template for this.

No playbook.

No knowledge repository.

I had to invent it.

And doing that — pulling order from chaos without a roadmap.

That's when consulting became my entire identity.

Because accomplishing something that hard and that improbable, in a system that broken, with so much pressure and so little guidance... it felt like becoming a man in real time.

The engagement partner became more than a mentor.

He became a friend.

A big brother.

A man I admired and loved. And still do.

A man who called something out of me that no one else had.

The consulting ecosystem with him was like combat — long stretches of tension punctuated by breakthroughs, late nights, existential pressure, impossible deadlines, all while delivering results that clients desperately needed. Only people who've lived in that world understand the bond it creates. It's forged in fire.

And somewhere in that fire, consulting became who I was.

Not a job.

Not a role.

An identity.

It gave me:

- belonging
- purpose
- validation
- structure
- direction
- self-worth
- a place to channel every drop of overachievement
- men I admired
- missions that mattered
- a sense that my mind could actually change things

I didn't know it then, but this was the beginning of both the ascent and the slow burn that would eventually consume me.

For now, though, I was finally somebody.

And I was addicted to that feeling.

Burnout

Burnout doesn't start as fire.

It starts as friction — the slow grinding of a man's soul against the machinery he was never built to serve.

Mine began after the Y2K rush evaporated and the consulting market headed straight toward a cliff. You could smell the desperation in the air —

firms puffing up proposals, partners fighting for scraps, capital calls, fear hanging over every hallway conversation.

I saw it coming.

I got out before the fall hit me.

I interviewed for a CFO role at a local real estate investment trust. "Interviewed" is too polite a word — I was put through a gauntlet. Cycles with the owner and president/CEO. Quantitative interviews. Writing samples. Strategy frameworks. And a half-day interrogation with an industrial psychiatrist who ran me through an IQ test and a full psychological profile.

It felt like they were dissecting me.

But I passed.

I took the role.

The First Crack

On my first day, I walked in expecting some semblance of corporate structure. Instead, I saw a fax machine vomiting paper onto the floor like a busted artery.

"What the hell is this?" I asked the controller.

"This is how we close our books," he said.

That was the first moment the ground tilted. I had stepped into a hybrid blue collar/ R&B culture filled with people who had heart but lacked discipline, systems, or the kind of financial rigor I had been trained in. A board member tried to micromanage me from day one — but even as a young CFO, I learned quickly to box him out.

I stabilized cash. I collected receivables with a vengeance.

Then I turned to implementing a new web-based accounting system to replace the fucking fax machine. A clean set of financials hadn't been produced in months and was built on sabotage — deleted journal entries, opening balances that didn't reconcile with closing ones. Someone wanted me to fail.

I kept going anyway. With the system in place and a newly hired accounting manager, the cleanup went quickly. I was making the tough calls that transformed the back office.

They gave me regional manager responsibilities. Dangled the COO track in front of me. Tried to shape me into their vision, not mine.

But the culture was rotten.

The ownership charged above market rents to the core business, and I had no way as a CFO to really measure results.

Nothing aligned with my values.

The final straw?

They demanded I fire the systems manager — the guy who had brought order out of chaos with me.

No.

Not for a job.

Not for anyone.

I left.

Without another job lined up.

And then a multinational technology consulting firm called.

The Blizzard

They put me on a business performance management strategy at a global consumer products manufacturer located on the east side of Lake Michigan — late fall — headed into a winter that felt Old Testament.

The client was hostile.

The visibility was enormous.

The work was abstract, oversold, and nearly impossible to scope.

I had two solid guys with me.

We were building the plane mid-air in a storm.

One night, mid-January, we walked out the front door of the corporate office.

A wall of white pitched against a black sky swallowed the parking lot.

My team literally disappeared into the blizzard — gone.

It took us ninety minutes to drive to Chili's for dinner. Ninety minutes for four miles.

Inside, thawing out with beers and exhaustion, I realized something:

Consulting wasn't about intelligence and doing great work anymore.

It was about surviving the next blow.

Satan himself was on the client roster — a man who took pleasure in diminishing my team, the corner of his mouth twitching with demonic satisfaction as he launched insults.

I tried to get him removed.

The client leadership didn't have the spine.

Five months later, the three of us wrapped the project in Chicago.

Drinks at the Intercontinental.

Dinner at Shaw's.

We felt like the survivors of a shipwreck — washed up, dazed, still breathing.

"That," I thought, "is the price you pay for oversold work."

You eat the hours.

You bleed for the deliverable.

You survive.

But something inside me dimmed.

The Political Years

I moved into selling big ERP strategy work — half-billion-dollar transformations full of politics that would make Machiavelli look like a kindergarten teacher.

I was screwed out of a bonus despite top ratings because the business unit as a whole didn't hit its target.

Fine. I left.

My first client at the new firm was a West Coast utility run by Stanford MBAs who measured human worth by pedigree. We were "Midwest," which made us inferior by default. The team they gave me was abysmal. The client hated us on sight.

Before the project even kicked off, I suffered a personal tragedy — one of those emotional ruptures that leaves a fault line in your soul. And at the kickoff meeting, it all hit at once.

I stood up — a simple move — to write something on the whiteboard just as I had done a million times before.

Suddenly I couldn't breathe.

The room folded.

My body slipped off itself.

My equilibrium crashed.

A panic attack.

Out of nowhere.

Like my nervous system had hit the eject button.

I looked at the partner, expecting him to catch me.

He didn't move.

He just watched.

Coldly.

Detached.

And at that moment, I knew:

My career at this firm was dead before it started.

But I salvaged the project anyway.

Sunday night flights in.

Red-eye flights out Thursday nights.

Straight to the office Friday mornings.

I bled for that project.

The client team gave me a standing ovation when I rolled off — but their leader smiled with just her teeth. Empty. Performative.

The Descent Begins

I left knowing the firm had already declared me a liability.

I got parked on a bullshit outsourcing job until I could rejoin my people who had moved to another global professional service firm.

By then, the stress had hollowed me out.

My coping mechanisms had shifted from habits to compulsions.

One day in tech support, sitting beside a young woman diagnosing my PC, my browser cache popped open.

A mile-long list of porn sites.

Everything I'd been hiding — exposed in one click.

I froze.

She laughed.

"Oh, you consultants... you're all the same."

Maybe some were.

But I wasn't "the same."

I was drowning.

Porn wasn't thrill.

It was anesthesia.

Workouts went.

Sleep went.

Breakfast went.

Self-respect went.

Then came strip clubs.

Shot glasses.

Twenty-dollar bills in a rainstorm.

Champagne rooms.

The smell of sex and stripper perfume clinging to my skin as I stumbled into the Marriott at 3 a.m.

I woke up at 7:15.

Interview at 8:00 with an EVP.

Jumped in the shower.

Hit the freeway at 100 mph.

Missed the exit.

Blew through the median.

Dirt, grass, and rocks flying.

Pulled into the client's office on time.

Sat down.

Delivered flawlessly.

The Breaking Years

This Big Four practice promised "large-scale process work," not ERP delivery. Perfect for me: former CFO, CPA, process guy.

But the practice wasn't selling.

My so-called coach was arrogant, hollow, and drunk on buzzwords.

She sat with her head back, glasses down her nose, performing superiority like a stage actress.

"We need to be our best selves," she said.

I stared at her and thought:

You're the fakest person I've ever met.

When I asked if she was going to recommend I get fired — with two kids, a mortgage, car payments, and a soft market — she didn't even flinch.

That was fear.

I moved into a brutal proposal — 100-hour weeks, we lost. The partner figuratively "running" the proposal had already checked out because he was retiring and was flippant with the prospective client at orals.

Then Global Automotive Manufacturer #2 called.

Still recovering from the long hours of the failed proposal effort, I woke at Noon and proceeded to the nearest Taco Bell for lunch.

"Are you chargeable?"

"No."

"You want to be?"

"I need to be."

"Get out here."

I put on a blazer.

Walked into the client.

They loved me.

They always did — in person.

I took over management reporting — the most delayed workstream in a massive SAP rollout. Due to the integrated nature of the work, two hundred people were waiting for my workstream's design. The burn rate added to the pressure. Another consulting firm — my old colleagues — were the implementation partner, trying to undermine me, discredit me, and steal the design work.

I worked every day for months.

Two young killers on my team.

I set the strategy.

I designed the master data.

We crushed it.

The work went global.

Tokyo.

Late nights. Different time zones.

Design harmonization sessions.

Whiskey at the Park Hyatt.

The client wanting me to run the entire finance implementation — even though I wasn't in the SAP practice.

Resentment everywhere.

Four years on that client.

No boundaries.

Calls nights and weekends.

One hundred people on the team.

Pressure that would snap most men.

And my compulsions escalated to extremes that made Caligula look restrained.

I won't detail them- they don't deserve oxygen.

I was losing myself.

The Exit

I got pulled into the Managing Director process.

I wrote and pitched my business case to my sponsor while on vacation with my family at Rum Point in Cayman.

Everyone descended on the office and W in mid-town Atlanta.

I played Eminem in my headphones before walking into the first session.

Not for swagger — for survival.

Panels with senior partners where you had twenty minutes to pitch your entire existence.

Partner dinners.

Cocktail hour with HR watching, quantifying, and scoring every movement.

I made it.

Promoted.

But the work dried up.

Finance transformation got cannibalized by new service lines.

Partners stole sales credit for deals they never touched.

The politics became cannibalistic.

Then my back started to fail- I had to have surgery and wound up being out of the office on short-term disability.

Three months later, I returned.

Three months after that, COVID hit.

After a ten-year run, I was one of the first people let go.

And I felt... relieved.

The culture had rotted.

Brilliance replaced by politics.

Teamwork replaced by self-preservation.

Community replaced by DEI theater.

Sincerity replaced by Gen Z platitudes.

The consulting world no longer resembled the one I entered.

I no longer resembled the man who entered it.

The Empty Search for Meaning

In the weeks after I left, my body crashed. Not the familiar crash after a big project where you've been running on adrenaline for months and then finally get a weekend to sleep it off. This was different. There was no Monday morning coming. No deck to deliver. No fire drill waiting in the inbox.

And that's when the thinking started.

I'd always wanted to get in a car and drive west — no plan, no itinerary, no deliverables — just point the hood toward the interior states and keep going until the landscape swallowed me. So that's exactly what I did. I trailered my Ducati Monster through Indiana, Illinois, Iowa, Nebraska... and when I crossed into Wyoming I felt something I hadn't felt in decades: space. I could breathe.

I passed the Continental Divide like I was shedding an old skin. I filled those long hours with podcasts — UFO theories, lost civilizations, exercise science, sauna protocols, cold plunge studies, supplements, unexplained mysteries. I devoured every sentence. I felt like someone had opened a window in a sealed room I'd been trapped in.

Wyoming bled into Yellowstone. I rode my Monster through landscapes that felt like another planet. I stopped by the Yellowstone River, at the plaque marking part of the Trail of Tears. One of my childhood heroes was Chief Joseph — I must've read that book a dozen times. Standing there, on that ground, bridging the story of their suffering with the chaos of my own childhood... it hit me like a punch. Their suffering made mine feel small and monumental at the same time. It put everything into proportion — the brutality, the endurance, the quiet dignity.

I rented a cabin in the park. Woke the next morning to a buffalo standing six feet from me like some prehistoric guardian. Slipped out into the cold to walk the steaming mud pots and sulfur vents before sunrise. That night I camped in a tent — two sleeping bags, temps dropping near 30 degrees. I hadn't slept that deeply since an overnight in Bangalore after being awake for almost 48 hours on a project. There's something about total exhaustion plus complete silence that reaches down and flips a breaker inside you.

From there I dropped into Utah — Moab, Arches, Canyonlands. The red rock felt alive. Eroded temples. Cathedrals carved by wind and time. I rode my Monster through the center of all of it, yelling four-letter words into my helmet because language wasn't enough to hold the beauty. Then Zion — which made everything else look like a warm-up act. I had been to many countries, seen a lot of "impressive" things, but Zion was something else entirely. Otherworldly. Mythic. Holy in a way the church never was.

The Grand Canyon, by comparison, felt almost anticlimactic. Petrified Forest. A night in Flagstaff visiting an old friend. And then the long-haul home — 23 hours straight because I didn't feel like stopping. That's the thing about trips like this: the more awe you drink in, the harder it is to return to the life you left.

And when I got home, the compulsions came roaring back.

I tried everything — diet, exercise, Bible reflection — none of it cut through the static. I went on NoFap with a friend. Didn't last. I relapsed coming home after the January 6th event in DC. I left early because it was oddly boring. Peaceful. Over a million people standing around listening to speeches. On the drive home I heard the reports from the Capitol. What weighed on me wasn't politics — it was the feeling that everything around me was a lie. My country. My career. My own brain.

Even travel wasn't enough to outrun it. So, I tried working again. A small strategy firm — friends of mine — tossed me a couple of projects.

Easy work. Boring. Nothing like the complex, high-stakes transformations I used to lead.

Then came another free-lance job. North America integration lead for a BPO program. I walked into a mess. The partner who sold the work had no idea how to deliver it. She ran 6 a.m. calls every morning, belittled the team, micromanaged out of fear, lashed out because she was in over her head. Treated me like a junior when I had shipped work she couldn't even diagram on a whiteboard. It wasn't ego — it was clarity. She was incompetent. The whole project was a con.

And I realized: I didn't need to put up with this shit anymore.

I took the stack of 500,000 $1 bills I was supposed to earn and set it on fire — figuratively — and walked. No hesitation. No second-guessing. Freedom tastes like that.

I took a few more trips. Then I turned toward home and the physical world. Built an entirely new bathroom in the basement for my sauna. Renovated two more. Rebuilt the laundry room. It was grounding — working with my hands, seeing immediate feedback instead of pushing pixels around for ungrateful clients who confuse PowerPoint for intelligence.

But even with all the space, the guilt and shame still lived deep inside me — so deep I didn't even know how far back it went. Uncertainty crept in. The market was still ice-cold. White-collar recession. No opportunities. Too much time to think.

"If I could snap my fingers and disappear, I would."

I felt unworthy of the animals that died to keep me fed.

Unworthy of my career.

Unworthy of purpose.

Just unworthy.

Not an example you want to set for two amazing kids.

Depression. Loneliness. Compulsions.

Anyone who's been in therapy knows the cycle — destructive, self-feeding, inescapable.

I tried before to white-knuckle my way out a hundred times.

The longer I abstained, the worse the rebound became.

I couldn't think my way out.

Human willpower wasn't enough.

Not even the Bible could pry loose whatever was gripping me.

I bought Viktor Frankl.

I read it in one day.

To watch a man stripped of dignity, starved, tortured, surrounded by unthinkable suffering — and still find purpose? Still choose meaning? Still rise internally when everything external was annihilated?

It shook something loose in me.

And that's when I sat down and drew the diagram that finally cracked open the beginning of my recovery.

The moment the collapse window started to close.

The moment the reckoning began.

Defining Stuck

There was always a strange comfort for me in the smell of a whiteboard marker in a team room—the clean friction of ink on a massive wall-sized board, the feeling that if I could just diagram the problem, I could solve the damn thing. When I hit the bottom and couldn't think my way out, I did the only thing my consulting brain knew how to do.

I defined stuck.

Tendency to overthink.

Can't get traction.

Leaving all options open.

No structure.

No flow.

Fear disguised as indecision.

I wrote it all down because I needed to see it outside of myself. I needed to look at the thing that had been running me from behind the curtain for decades. That's when I grabbed a pen and drew the first map of my collapse on a scrap of notebook paper—crude, uneven, nothing more than circles and arrows. But it was the first thing I had produced in months that felt true.

Chapter Three

THE DOPAMINE ECONOMY

Before Silicon Valley learned how to turn human attention into an extractive industry... before the smartphone became a tether carried in every pocket... before algorithms learned your patterns more precisely than your family ever could... there was the cigarette.

Not the romanticized cigarette you see in old movies. I'm talking about the engineered cigarette — the one designed in labs by people who knew exactly what they were doing and proceeded anyway.

The cigarette industry was the first modern institution to perfect engineered addiction. It was the birthplace of behavioral manipulation as a business model. Long before anyone talked about "engagement metrics" or "user retention," these companies were quietly perfecting how to control the rhythms of the human brain.

They didn't guess how addiction worked.

They measured it.

Refined it.

Optimized it.

Systematized it.

Monetized it.

Chemists altered burn rates so nicotine hit your bloodstream faster — dopamine spikes measured in seconds, not minutes. Psychologists mapped craving curves and emotional triggers. Marketers attached identity and rebellion and sex appeal to the act itself. And lawyers buried the truth so deeply that generations never knew what hit them.

They weren't selling tobacco.

They were selling dependence.

My grandfather smoked Lucky Strikes until it killed him at fifty-six. Even on his death bed, I'm told, he was still lighting up. It never occurred to me that addiction could be this powerful — powerful enough that even as it destroys people, they defend it.

But that's the truth: the addiction was so strong that smokers never wanted the product legislated out of existence. They accepted the risk because the next hit felt non-negotiable.

And that's what shocked me when I finally learned how cigarettes were engineered: human beings, under the banner of quarterly profits, could legally produce something that would kill millions... and do it without remorse.

Everything that came next — the modern dopamine economy — was built on that foundation.

The cigarette industry had to generalize addiction across populations. Tech companies don't. They personalize it. They tailor it. They refine it at the level of "you."

Your pauses.

Your cravings.

Your loneliness cycles.

Your search history.

Your micro-hesitations.

Your triggers.

Your vulnerabilities.

Your impulses.

Your 2 AM patterns.

Cigarettes were a shotgun.

Your phone is a sniper rifle.

And once you see this clearly, you understand the truth:

You're not a consumer. You're being **farmed**.

The Machinery of Extraction

The powerful don't look out at society and see human beings. They see markets. Behavioral clusters. Data cohorts. Segments. Risk surfaces. Retention curves.

They don't smell the rain on a warm night in Columbus.

They don't notice the look in a child's eyes.

They don't think in terms of dignity, or sorrow, or story.

They think in terms of behavioral predictability.

Attention becomes soil — stripped, mined, tilled, and harvested for profit until nothing is left.

And here's the truth behind the design:

Fear keeps eyes on screens.

Anger fuels engagement.

Loneliness creates consumption.

Insecurity drives purchasing.

Stress keeps dopamine demand high.

Despair keeps people inside loops.

The dopamine economy didn't evolve naturally.

It wasn't an accident of innovation.

It was built.

Normalized.

Scaled.

Weaponized.

A multi-trillion-dollar system created by people who understand how the human nervous system works — and how to target it with precision.

Behavioral economists, neuroscientists, machine learning experts, UX psychologists — an entire army of specialists working not on curing disease or helping the human spirit grow, but on perfecting the architecture of craving.

The goal isn't fulfillment.

The goal is repetition.

You don't have to be happy.

You just have to keep coming back.

And the system is built to make sure you do.

The Moment I Saw the Pattern

I used to think my compulsivity was about desire.

In truth, it was about pattern.

A learned, reinforced, predictable pattern.

Stress triggered it.

Boredom triggered it.

Loneliness triggered it.

Achievement triggered it.

A hard day... a good day... a neutral day... it didn't matter.

If I was awake, the pull was there.

The news cycle was one of the easiest ways to fall in. I would look for something dark or infuriating — something to feel bad about — and then chase a hit to escape the tension I just created. A loop made of misery on the front end and dopamine on the back end.

For a long time, I called it desire. But deep down I knew better. Especially on the road, in hotel rooms. I saw the loneliness in myself — and in other men — so clearly. I remember a consulting night where a senior manager checked out of a Marriott with twenty movies on his bill. Twenty. I thought: "Who can watch twenty movies in one night?"

And then it clicked.

This wasn't entertainment.

It was escape.

The loop felt like a tunnel. Once I stepped in, I was committed. Laser-focused, fully dissociated from the rest of my life. Not mechanical — emotional, even hopeful — but detached from reality. Expecting reciprocation, connection, relief. Anything to short-circuit the ache.

And then there was another night where I walked into a strip club and withdrew a fistful of cash from the house ATM. I knew the address would appear on the bank statement and someone at home was likely to notice. The risk was identified but never calculated. I remember looking at the cash in my hand and thinking... this isn't me.

And yet it was.

This was the part of me that ran when I wasn't awake.

It wasn't moral failure.

It was circuitry.

Chapter Four

THE FALSE FEMININE

I was five years old the first time my nervous system found a way out. The magazine came from Caveman Jim's place — that house in the neighborhood where kids roamed around unsupervised and adults were just… there, orbiting in their own chaos. I didn't steal it with intent. I just found it, brought it home, and hid it in the loft above our garage. I tucked it into the center of a rolled-up carpet like I was hiding contraband from the world, even though I didn't know what I was hiding or why it mattered.

That loft was nothing special: rough beams, fiberglass insulation, the smell of old wood and oil. But it was quiet. Suspended. Separate. Removed from whatever emotional static lived downstairs. Climbing up there felt like stepping into a world where the tension in my body could actually loosen for a moment. I didn't understand the images in that magazine. I didn't even really look at them for what they were. What I felt was the first moment of quiet my nervous system had ever known. My breathing slowed. The hum of vigilance eased.

People like to talk about early exposure as if it's about curiosity or desire. It's neither. Not at that age. It's about relief. It's about the first time your body stops bracing. It's about silence inside your own skin. You don't forget that. You can't. It imprints on you before you even know what imprinting is.

A kid who grows up wrapped in real warmth doesn't crawl into a loft at five years old to find peace in something he doesn't understand. But my house wasn't warm. It wasn't cold, either. That's the part people misunderstand. If it had been cold, I could've made sense of it. The problem was that it looked warm. It looked loving. On the surface, there were all the markers of a close family: soft voices, Christian virtue, nostalgia, holiday memories, stories told with gentle affection. No screaming. No hitting. No dramatic scenes. Everything looked just fine.

But nothing landed.

Because underneath all that sentimentality was an emotional emptiness that nobody talked about, maybe because nobody knew how to name it. Affection existed in form, not substance. Closeness existed in proximity, not in presence. Love existed in words, not in resonance. I grew up in what felt like a play — the gestures were there, but the energy wasn't. Nothing settled my nervous system. Nothing made me feel safe. Nothing gave my body the signal, "You're held. You're seen."

And here's the part that explains everything: my subconscious already knew the truth.

My body remembered what had happened to me long before my mind could process it. That's how the nervous system works. It records danger. It encodes betrayal. It builds rules meant for survival. Long before I understood anything consciously, my body had already made its decision: "I am not safe here."

So even when my mother appeared to try to be tender, something in me stiffened. Even when moments looked affectionate, nothing in me opened. Even when love was offered, the part of me that needed it most rejected it because my nervous system couldn't take in comfort from the same person it associated with danger. That's the kind of fracture childhood trauma creates — a split between what you're told is happening and what your body knows is true.

My mother's own story explains some of that fracture. She grew up in Meigs County, one of the poorest corners of Ohio — a place where life was more about surviving than living. Her father drank heavily and smoked nonstop, a man who had been hollowed out by his own pain long before she was born. Tenderness wasn't something he knew how to give. Her siblings were raised in the same environment, all of them enduring more than they received. She was singled out the most — teased for an eye condition, humiliated by poverty, burdened by shame that didn't belong to her.

There were deeper wounds too, the kind you don't speak of because language isn't enough to hold them. Trauma changes a child. It changes their body, their ability to trust, their instinct to attach. The way she clung to religion because the alternative was acknowledging pain without a roadmap.

When she found Christian Science at seventeen, it must have felt like salvation. A belief system that told her suffering wasn't real? That pain could be erased through "right thinking?" That the body itself was an illusion? Of course she clung to that. It gave her a way to survive her past without confronting it.

But a belief system built on denial can't raise a child.

So I grew up with a mother who couldn't connect on a human level. She was overly sentimental without attunement, affectionate without safety, soft without grounding. My father wasn't the villain, but he wasn't the anchor either — and that's a story for another chapter. The emotional center of my childhood was a kind of hollow warmth: a home that might have looked loving on the outside but didn't reach my nervous system on the inside.

And when a boy cannot accept comfort from the person who hurt him, he learns to find comfort somewhere else.

I didn't choose the loft.

My nervous system did.

It chose the one place where relief didn't come attached to betrayal.

That's the origin of the False Feminine.

It wasn't lust.

It wasn't thrill.

It wasn't curiosity.

It was self-preservation.

What I didn't understand for a long time is that this wasn't just psychological.

It was physiological.

When arousal is repeatedly paired with novelty, escalation, and artificial cues, the brain learns those associations. Real intimacy — slower, reciprocal, embodied — can begin to feel muted or effortful by comparison.

This is not loss of masculinity.

It is conditioning.

The nervous system learned what it was repeatedly taught.

Perhaps the most subtle effect is the hardest to name.

Over time, reward becomes disconnected from effort, risk, presence, or relationship. Pleasure arrives without cost. Relief arrives without connection.

Life continues to function — work, family, reputation — but it begins to feel hollow. Accomplishments don't register. Gratitude feels forced. The world loses texture.

This isn't depression in the traditional sense.

It's depletion.

The system has been trained for intensity, not depth.

The False Feminine is not a woman. It's the imitation of feminine presence — the appearance of warmth without the risk of closeness. It shows up in imagery, in fantasy, in the curated world of adult content, in the faces and bodies used to sell a feeling that looks like intimacy but asks nothing of you. It is feminine energy stripped of soul, of reciprocity, of depth. It's connection without relationship. It's intensity without vulnerability. At first, it's comfort without danger.

And for someone like me — someone whose body rejected maternal closeness because it encoded danger in the same breath as love — the False Feminine felt safer than the real thing.

As I moved into adolescence, the wiring deepened. I didn't know how to talk to real girls. I didn't feel chosen. I didn't feel confident. I was thin, anxious, socially off to the side. I had no stable ground inside myself to stand on. So I turned toward the one place where my nervous system didn't brace. The False Feminine became the proxy for connection.

Not because I was perverted.

Because I was alone.

Porn became the emotional surrogate for the mothering I never received. It never rejected me. It never withdrew. It never contradicted itself. It never smiled and then froze. It never said one thing and felt another. It didn't confuse my subconscious. It didn't remind my body of danger.

It was predictable.

And predictability, when you grow up with emotional betrayal, feels like love.

As time passed, the loop deepened. My brain learned the ritual. The anticipation. The relief. The reward. The isolation. The shame. The reset.

Again and again, carving a trench so deep it would follow me into adulthood.

When you expose a child's brain to adult-level intensity too early, the wiring changes instantly. The dopamine system imprints the relief as safety. The limbic system attaches to the ritual as comfort. The prefrontal cortex — the brakes — doesn't even exist yet. Fantasy becomes the regulator instead of connection. Intimacy is replaced by intensity long before intimacy even has a chance to develop. Shame arrives before you even understand what you're ashamed of.

That's the tragedy. Your innocence doesn't leave. It gets overwritten.

As I grew older, the False Feminine escalated the way all addictions escalate. Magazines turned into videos. Videos into interactive content. Interactive content into physical encounters. And before long, I was walking into situations no sane adult should walk into — in houses where I shouldn't have been, with people I didn't know, in moments that could have ended my life. I wasn't reckless. I was conditioned. The earliest wiring in my nervous system was running the show.

From Playboy to the Digital Inferno

Long before I ever fell into the trap, the trap was already built. Before the internet, before webcams, before infinite access and algorithmic temptation, three men laid the foundation for an entire sexual economy: Hugh Hefner, Bob Guccione, and Larry Flynt. They didn't invent the False Feminine — they industrialized it. They turned it from a private vice into a cultural operating system.

What they understood—decades before neuroscience caught up—is that men aren't addicted to sex. Men are addicted to the appearance of feminine approval. They realized that if you could create a product that makes a man feel desired, admired, accepted, validated, and wanted—even superficially—you could bypass the deepest emotional wounds inside him. You could reach the part of the male nervous system that aches for closeness but has no idea how to ask for it.

So they created a feminine persona that was endlessly available, endlessly approving, eternally youthful, incapable of disappointment, untouched by trauma, uncomplicated, unburdened, unscarred. It was a feminine aesthetic without feminine soul. A mask without a heartbeat. Intimacy stripped of humanity and packaged as stimulation. That was the original False Feminine. And men consumed it because they were starving long before anyone talked about attachment wounds or emotional neglect or spiritual numbness.

Hefner and his competitors didn't need a psychologist to explain what was happening. They watched the sales numbers. They saw the hunger. They saw how easily men folded into an illusion of approval. They understood that most men were walking around with quiet despair—emotional hunger, unresolved childhood wounds, sexually disconnected marriages, shame around desire, boredom, loneliness they didn't have words for. They built an empire not on compassion or innovation, but on predation disguised as glamour.

And then the internet came along and poured gasoline on the fire.

What was once limited, slow, and imagination-driven suddenly became infinite, on-demand, personalized, and optimized. The False Feminine didn't just scale—it mutated. It evolved from a static fantasy into a neurological feedback loop. No wait times. No friction. No boundaries. Just bottomless novelty—the single strongest dopamine trigger known to the human brain.

But the final evolutionary stage—the nuclear-grade version—was webcams. AI is now taking this to the point of fueling the collapse of the human being.

This changed everything.

The False Feminine didn't just perform. It responded. It mirrored. It looked into the camera and said your name. It activated a part of the male nervous system that pornography alone could never touch: the attachment system. Suddenly a collapsing man—emotionally empty, spiritually numb, overwhelmed by life—wasn't just getting sexual stimulation. He was getting the illusion of being seen. He was getting emotional mimicry. He was getting pseudo-connection.

Webcams didn't target lust—they targeted loneliness.

That's the psychological mismatch built into modern compulsion: men are seeking connection; transactional sexuality sells stimulation. The two realities never overlap. But the illusion feels close enough to pass for the real thing, and close enough to replace what's missing in a man's actual life.

By the time my descent ever started, the ecosystem was already waiting for me. The fantasy, the validation, the attention, the pseudo-intimacy, the curated feminine persona, the dopamine spike, the shame loop, the secrecy, the collapse—it was all engineered long before I walked through the door.

I wasn't stepping into a mistake.

I was stepping into a machine.

A system that understood men far better than men understood themselves.

A system that didn't care who it devoured.

The Lie at the Heart of All Transactional Sex

Transactional sexuality can never understand the world a collapsing man is speaking from — not because the people inside it are bad or stupid, but because the entire ecosystem operates on a completely different psychological operating system.

Anyone performing inside transactional sex — whether it's porn, camming, escorting, stripping, or even casual seduction used for leverage — is functioning within an economy built on performance, stimulation, immediacy, and attention. Everything is constructed around the emotional surface. Persona matters more than presence. Arousal matters more than authenticity. Predictability matters more than depth.

It's an industry designed for stimulation, not intimacy — response without relationship, mask without vulnerability, imagery without soul. The performer is rewarded for staying above their own wounds, not descending into them. Emotional distance becomes a skill. Vulnerability becomes a liability. Depth is irrelevant. Understanding is unnecessary.

But transactional sexuality has no bandwidth for any of that. It can only offer the appearance of intimacy, never the weight of it.

So the man brings his wounds, and the performer brings her persona. These two realities do not intersect. They don't even live in the same psychological universe. The man is speaking from decades of consequences; the performer is speaking from a system where consequences don't show up until years later. He is looking for connection; she is trained to deliver illusion. He is collapsing; the system is built to pretend collapse doesn't exist.

This is the core tragedy of the False Feminine: it perfectly imitates what a wounded man longs for, but it has zero capacity to deliver it. It is intimacy hollowed out. Desire without relationship. Connection without presence. Feminine energy without feminine soul.

It is the ultimate bait-and-switch for the male nervous system.

The Psychological Mismatch

There's a truth most men never articulate because they're too ashamed to admit they expected something real from something engineered to be hollow. The entire thing operates on a mismatch. A twenty-year-old cam girl can't understand the world a collapsing man is speaking from — she's not stupid or malicious, she's unformed. She's living inside an economy built on stimulation, validation, immediacy, and performance. Her nervous system is tuned to attention and reward loops. Her prefrontal cortex isn't even fully matured. She hasn't lived long enough to understand her own pain, let alone a man's.

She offers a performance.

He needs connection.

The False Feminine was never built for depth. It was built for immediacy. And this mismatch is what keeps millions of men trapped — trying to draw water from a well that was never built to have any depth in the first place.

Once I saw the truth, the persona — the mask — shattered.

The False Feminine died.

The ego scaffolding collapsed.

The compulsions lost their glamour.

I now understood the psychology and the spiritual reality behind what had ruled my life:

Chasing the False Feminine made me feel powerful for an hour and hollow for a week.

It propped up my ego while starving my soul.

It let me play the role of a man while never actually becoming one.

The parts of me that had to die were exactly the parts trauma had built:

- the belief that my worth came from work
- the belief that love was performance
- the belief that intimacy was conquest
- the belief that dopamine was meaning
- the belief that I was tragically flawed

Those lies had to die so the true man could emerge — the man God intended when He designed me.

Chapter Five

SYSTEMS FAILURE

The Collapse Space

There's a point where the body stops negotiating with you. Mine had been whispering warnings for years—fatigue, knots in my lower back, that tight electric hum of a nervous system stuck in fifth gear. I ignored it all. I piled on flights, sugar, porn, whiskey, fake intimacy, fake relationships, fake rest. I just kept pressing forward because that's what insecure overachievers do. We outrun the truth until the truth tackles us.

My moment came between L5 and S1. A ruptured disc, the kind surgeons shake their heads at. Pain that didn't fit on the scale—if a ten is screaming, this was a fifty. It shot down my leg like a live wire. I couldn't sit. I couldn't concentrate. I couldn't sleep. I couldn't even pretend to be okay. And the more it hurt, the more I acted out, trying to drown the pain with dopamine—sex, alcohol, anger, sugar, anything.

I spent two years like this. Standing in TSA lines, dropping to my knees, folding forward because it was the only way to ease the pain.

Concerned fellow travelers asking me if I were ok. "It's just my back."

I was flying back and forth to Los Angeles during that time carrying a body that was coming apart molecule by molecule. On one red-eye home, I drank more Jack Daniel's than I want to admit. The flight attendant became my target—another attempt to feel powerful when in reality I was disintegrating. I embarrassed myself. Not theatrically, just pathetically. When we landed, I staggered toward the exit—only to see someone on the project stepping onto the same plane for the turnaround flight. I muttered something casual because that's all I could muster. I should've been sharp, engaged, leading him into the week's strategy. Instead, I was a ghost in a suit, drowning in Jack and nerve pain.

That was the first moment I couldn't lie to myself anymore.

I wasn't doing my job.

And I knew it.

The earliest signs were all there long before that night. Constant fatigue. Micro-panic at the smallest things—body language in meetings, incompetent staff, unfair tasks, panicked clients. My fight-or-flight switch was stuck in "on," buzzing under my skin from the moment I woke up. I didn't know then what I know now: compulsive behavior drives inflammation, inflammation drives pain, pain drives more compulsive behavior. It's a perfect loop straight into hell.

Having to fly constantly was the worst-case scenario. That pressure change, the cramped seats, the endless sitting—every flight felt like torture. Literal torture. I could feel my spine screaming. I could feel my mind unraveling.

And then the fear crept in—the kind that attacks the life you built, not the body that built it.

Someone in my orbit turned vindictive. Fake Facebook pages. Anonymous posts on X. Attempts on LinkedIn. Threatening texts saying they would destroy me. That was when I understood what helplessness actually feels like: when someone else has a finger on the trigger of your life, and your entire career—your meticulously crafted veneer—can be blown apart with one rumor.

I went to the police. I should've gone sooner. But consulting culture is a sick performance: you're allowed to fail privately but never publicly. One bad meeting, one off day, one misstep, and you're branded. So you learn to hide everything. You pretend you're bulletproof until the bullets start landing.

And yet here I am now—writing a book.

Not hiding.

Not pretending.

Not performing.

I have no shame left about telling the truth. Shame requires secrecy, and I burned down the hiding places. The collapse stripped me clean. If anyone wants to judge me, let them.

The old belief—that my value came from being flawless, tireless, promotable, indispensable—died right there in the collapse. What came next wasn't wisdom yet, or awakening, or healing.

It was just clarity:

Something inside me was dying, and if I didn't change, the rest of me would go with it.

The Emotional and Psychological Drought

Burnout isn't just physical. Before the body collapses, the soul dries out. You don't notice it at first. You just start losing the *quality* of your emotions. You can still feel excitement, gratitude, anticipation — but they're thin, washed-out versions of what they used to be. Like someone drained all the color out of your inner world and left you with grayscale imitations.

I never stopped feeling. That's the lie people tell about burnout — that you go numb. No. I felt everything. I just couldn't feel anything **fully**. Even joy had static in it, like it was being played through a blown speaker. Gratitude felt transactional. Anticipation felt forced. And "love"... well, what I called love back then wasn't love at all.

I mistook love for *performance* — for what I could buy, provide, create, control. For what I could pull out of somebody with charm, money, intimacy, or access. I didn't understand that real love requires vulnerability. I was performing affection while being emotionally unreachable. A man with a steel door welded shut over his heart calling it connection.

The anger at home — these ridiculous overreactions to small things. A tone. A question. A dirty dish. Something trivial would set me off because my ego had swollen into this grotesque balloon I was carrying around. Consulting had inflated it. Acting out had inflated it. Success had inflated it. And all of it was built on sand.

What pissed me off most was that **I knew better.** I knew the man I wanted to be. I knew the father I already was. But the husband? The partner? The emotionally grounded man? He wasn't there. He wasn't even born yet. And the gap between intention and behavior was humiliating. Every overreaction, every collapse at home, every moment of misplaced rage was proof that something deep in me was fundamentally off.

Underneath it all was a quiet, corrosive form of pain: inadequacy.

Not professional inadequacy — I was excellent at my craft.

But existential inadequacy.

This industry breeds insecure overachievers, and I was its target customer from day one. You never feel good enough. You never feel "made." Even with a stellar career and real skills, there's always some invisible measuring stick telling you:

"You're not partner.""You're not top-tier enough."

"You're replaceable."

"You're only as valuable as your last win."

So you grind. You perform. You produce. You overdeliver. You bleed for the job. And at the end of the day, you still feel like you're coming up short.

That quiet pain — that low hum of internal deficiency — is the fuel source for burnout. It keeps the machine running long after the soul wants off the ride.

And in the silence beneath all of it lived a truth I refused to face: Something inside me had gone hollow.

And I was trying to fill it with all the wrong things.

The Masculine Collapse

There's a kind of collapse that doesn't show up in MRIs or bloodwork. It lives in the space between the man you're trying to be and the man you actually are. And when that gap gets too wide, something cracks.

Even in the middle of all the chaos, the compulsions, the shame, the ego, the exhaustion — my kids were the one place I didn't fail. I never missed their events. I saved early for their education. I made sure they grew up knowing what security felt like. Every night, before bed, I asked them the same two questions:

Do you feel safe?

Do you feel loved?

Those weren't clichés. They were course corrections — the questions I wish someone had asked *me* as a child. My sons were raised in combat sports because I wanted them to walk through the world with the physical confidence I never had. I wanted them to know they could take care of themselves in ways I couldn't at their age. In that arena, I was a provider and protector to the bone.

But as a husband?

Broken.

Utterly broken.

And what made it worse was that I didn't even know it at first. It's easy to feel competent in the areas where you shine. It's harder to face the places where your shadow is running the show. I didn't realize how emotionally stunted, disconnected, avoidant, and ego-protected I was until my early forties. By then, the patterns were welded into me.

People talk about masculinity like it's a set of roles — provider, protector, leader. But the real core of masculinity is integration: a man whose internal pieces are aligned, not splintered. My roles were intact. My integration was not.

I thought intimacy was a performance.

I thought sex was proof of worth.

I thought charm was connection.

I thought generosity was love.

In reality, I was just a man with a starving ego — feeding it dopamine hits from the False Feminine. Every compulsion inflated my ego. Every inflated moment made me more compulsive. That cycle built a false version of me: confident on the outside, hollowed out on the inside.

And then one day, it all stopped working.

Compulsion didn't soothe.

Sex didn't validate.

Ego didn't protect.

Dopamine didn't lift me.

It all collapsed under its own weight.

That's when I met the worst emotional state a man can face:

Stuck.

Stuck is not depression.

Stuck is not fear.

Stuck is not apathy.

Stuck is when you know — with terrifying clarity — that the life you're living is not your real life, but you can't see the path to the one you were meant for. You're not dying, but you're not really alive either. You're suspended in a moral and spiritual purgatory where every instinct in you screams:

Move.

Change.

Break something open.

Get out.

But you don't.

You just keep existing.

And in those moments, the darkest lie creeps in:

There must be something permanently wrong with me.

For years, I believed that. I thought I was "tragically flawed." But here's the truth that only came later:

There was never anything wrong with me.

There was only an intersection —

my DNA, my upbringing, my childhood trauma, my coping patterns, my environment — colliding with a culture engineered to farm men like me for dopamine.

I wasn't flawed.

I was wired for survival.

And survival had outlived its usefulness.

The real problem wasn't defect — it was misalignment.

The man God designed and the man I had become were two different creatures entirely.

And that gap... that fracture... that quiet sense of being a fraud in your own skin...that is what breaks a man long before the world ever sees it.

Spiritual Exhaustion

Burnout hits the body first, the emotions second, the mind third.

But the final frontier — the quiet death that almost no one talks about — is spiritual exhaustion.

For most of those years, my relationship with God was shaped by Christian Science. Not the people — the framework. It's metaphysical, intellectual, abstract. It teaches you to treat compulsions as "unreal," to deny their substance, to see everything painful as error rather than injury. And my mind could run that loop all day long. It made sense to me because it allowed me to stay in control. If everything painful was unreal, then nothing had to change.

But the truth is, Christian Science left me spiritually cold.

Not hateful.

Not rebellious.

Just... untouched.

Their lesson sermons pulled fragments from everywhere in the Bible — a verse from here, a verse from there, all threaded together by commentary from "Science and Heath." Jesus wasn't a man who walked the earth. He was an abstraction — "the Christ," the metaphysical symbol of truth, immortality, perfection. Something to contemplate, not someone to encounter.

And when your soul is collapsing, abstractions don't hold you.

I never felt beyond redemption.

Even in the worst moments.

Not because I felt holy — but because I knew that as long as I was still breathing, God wasn't done with me. But I did live in the delusion of **tomorrow**:

"Just one more time, then tomorrow I'll stop."

"Tomorrow I'll get serious."

"Tomorrow I'll be better."

But tomorrow never comes for a man who refuses to move his feet.

It finally hit me: The greatest sin wasn't lust or anger or compulsion.

The greatest sin was wasting my life — *standing in the middle of a path God never meant me to die on.*

Spiritual exhaustion wasn't God abandoning me.

It was God stripping me bare.

Taking the junk heap of a car that was my life — rusted, dented, smoke pouring out — and tearing it down to metal so He could rebuild it the way it was meant to run.

Therapy didn't save my life.

Neuroscience didn't save my life.

God saved my life.

And He used every tool — Scripture, trauma work, nutrition, cold plunge, sauna, science, discipline — to do it.

What I didn't understand then but see clearly now is this:

God wasn't punishing me.

He was pruning me.

He was burning out the rot.

He was preparing me for the life I was born to live.

Spiritual exhaustion wasn't the end.

It was the turning.

The quiet, sacred death before resurrection.

Daily Life During Systems Failure

Systems failure isn't just a moment.

It's a daily ecosystem — a world you wake up inside and can't escape, no matter how hard you try. The tragedy isn't the explosions. It's the routine.

I woke up with dread every single morning. Even on weekends. Before I checked my phone. Before I opened my eyes. It was just *there*, floating in my body like a black fog waiting to smother the day before it started. It felt like my soul had been dipped in a vat of depression. Not the dramatic kind — the quiet kind that devours your internal light molecule by molecule.

People can live with fear. People can live with shame.

But dread is a different animal.

Dread tells you that your life is fundamentally misaligned. That you're walking the earth as someone you were never meant to be.

Sleep didn't help, because sleep barely existed. Nights were a different kind of battle. I would toss and turn, chasing a comfortable position that didn't exist. My body refused to calm. Not my mind — my *body.* The adrenaline, the inflammation, the unhealed trauma, the compulsions — kept me wired long after the world fell quiet.

I didn't stay awake because I was worrying.

I stayed awake because my system didn't know how to shut down.

So I grew to dread both ends of the day: I dreaded waking up. And I dreaded going to sleep.

There's a special kind of madness in that — when both the entrance and exit of the day feel hostile.

Work didn't collapse all at once. I white-knuckled it for a long time. Decades of consulting had trained me to deliver under any conditions — pain, exhaustion, depression, travel, chaos, you name it. But eventually even that cracked. My practice fell apart. The guy who built it got fired. Other service lines cannibalized what we'd created. The market shifted, and instead of doing high-impact work, I found myself on accounts no one wanted — or worse, on accounts trying to steal sold work from other firms.

Milwaukee.

Of all places.

I remember sitting in a rental car in Milwaukee, staring at my laptop, knowing the game was over. I wasn't adding value. I wasn't inspired. I wasn't aligned. I was just... filling space. Taking up a seat until someone finally had the courage to say what we all knew: I didn't belong there anymore.

And the truth?

By that time, I didn't give a fuck.

That's how you know burnout isn't a mood — it's a collapse of meaning. When a man stops caring about the craft he once tied his identity to, the soul is giving a warning shot.

Get out. Change course. Or die inside.

And beneath all this was the smallest but heaviest truth:

I didn't actually want to do anything.

Not chores.

Not errands.

Not responsibilities.

Not tasks.

Nothing.

It wasn't laziness. It was the collapse of internal drive. When the nervous system is fried, even basic life maintenance feels like trying to lift concrete blocks underwater. I could do the big things — deliver to clients, show up for my sons, manage a project — but the small things? The ones that depend on internal self-regulation? Those felt impossible.

My willpower had been spent.

My brain chemistry shot.

My routines corrupted.

My body screaming.

The only thing I consistently chose was the one thing that was destroying me: **acting out.**

Compulsion was the only predictable relief — until it wasn't relief anymore. Until it became just another room in the prison. And once I was in that loop, the days blurred, one identical to the next:

Wake up with dread → grind through work → hold it together for my sons → collapse into compulsion → lie awake unable to sleep → start again.

It was a life on repeat.

A man on autopilot.

A body moving without a soul.

And yet — even then — even in the thickest part of the fog — a small truth was forming underneath:

I wasn't meant to live like this.

I knew it.

I just didn't know how to stop.

The Breaking Point

Every collapse has a moment when the old version of you realizes it's dying. Not metaphorically. Literally. The self you've been carrying around — the ego, the compulsions, the identity, the illusions — starts coming apart like a structure whose beams have finally rotted through.

For me, that moment wasn't dramatic.

It wasn't a breakdown.

It wasn't tears on the bathroom floor.

It wasn't a crisis call or an ambulance or a panic attack.

It was **clarity**.

Not peace.

Not revelation.

Just cold, surgical clarity:

I cannot live this way anymore.

People imagine transformation starts with inspiration. It doesn't.

It starts with a verdict.

I walked into that theater carrying the man I thought I was, and I walked out carrying the truth of the man I actually was. I don't know how else to describe it. Something in me snapped into place. I felt owned by that moment — like God held my face in His hands and said:

"Pay attention. This is your life. Wake up."

I'm someone who has to be fully bought in.

Half-measures don't move me.

Ambivalence is useless.

I need conviction in my bones before I change anything.

A line drawn in the sand:

No more.

Not like this.

Not one more day.

And with that clarity came a second truth I didn't expect: I didn't care if the veneer cracked anymore.

The polished, successful, high-status consulting identity — the one I'd spent decades constructing — collapsed in a single instant. I didn't care who knew what. I didn't care what broke open. I didn't care if I died penniless. I wasn't here to perform anymore. I wasn't here to maintain a façade. I wasn't here to impress anyone — family, peers, clients, neighbors, strangers.

I was done pretending.

What pushed me toward the edge wasn't one event. It was the accumulation of a decade of misalignment.

- No meaning.
- No purpose.
- No internal north star.
- And no desire for anything offered by the world I had built.

I didn't want to die — but I didn't want to be here either.

That's a distinction most people never articulate. It isn't suicidal ideation. It's existential starvation. It's the sense that you are occupying a life that should have belonged to someone else.

The most dangerous wilderness a man can enter is the moment when he stops wanting anything at all.

I found joy in nothing.

I felt purpose in nothing.

Money meant nothing.

Success meant nothing.

Pleasure meant nothing.

The irony is that during my darkest moment, my body was the strongest it had ever been.

I had a cold plunge.

A sauna.

A tight diet.

A consistent workout routine.

I was lean, powerful, disciplined — physically.

But spiritually?

Emotionally?

Psychologically?

I was running on fumes.

It's almost funny now: I didn't know why I bought the plunge and sauna back then. I thought I was just optimizing. But those were survival tools before I understood the neuroscience. Grace hidden inside Amazon orders.

My body didn't collapse.

My mind didn't collapse.

My spirit did.

And that was the beginning of liberation — because once a man sees the truth of his internal condition, he cannot unsee it. He cannot go back to sleep. He cannot pretend that the life he built is the life he is meant to die in.

The breaking point wasn't an end.

It was a door.

And the only way through was destruction —

of ego, of compulsion, of identity, of the false self.

The Collapse of the Family of Origin Narrative

Every man who burns out at the soul level is carrying something older than adulthood. Burnout isn't caused by consulting hours or travel or stress. Those are accelerants. The real ignition source is buried in childhood — in the original fractures that taught you how to survive, how to adapt, how to hide, how to cope.

For me, the truth was simple and brutal: **My collapse didn't start in my twenties.**

It started when I was an infant.

And I didn't want that story.

No son wants to believe that the woman who raised him is also the one who damaged him.

But denial is expensive.

It keeps you loyal to the wrong story.

It keeps you blaming yourself for symptoms that began before you could talk.

My mother's behavior wasn't eccentric or "just her personality." It was psychological warfare — subtle, invasive, boundary-shattering, impossible for a child to name.

She betrayed confidences.

She intruded on private spaces.

She weaponized affection.

She violated boundaries in ways that looked invisible to outsiders but felt corrosive to a child's identity.

There was that Easter dinner. We had told her privately that we were expecting — keeping it quiet because of a previous heart-breaking midterm miscarriage. My mother stood at that holiday table and announced it as if it was her news to expose. Nothing about it was excitement. It was control.

And when she first heard we were expecting again, she responded coldly: "Well, I hope it works this time." Who says that to their son?

There was the bathroom incident — my oldest was three. I took him into the men's room at church. My mother saw us go in. She walked through the other door — into the men's room — and entered the stall area like the moment belonged to her.

There was the day my second son was born. I was in the hospital room, and the baby was being nursed. I moved to shut the door for privacy. It wouldn't close. I looked down — her foot was in the doorjamb. I looked up — she was peering inside.

Not maternal.

Not loving.

Something else entirely.

Something that erodes a child's sense of self.

I once told my aunt, "Every time I'm around her, I feel like I have an anaconda wrapped around my chest." My aunt said, "She doesn't hate you," but she didn't offer an explanation — because she didn't have one.

The truth is this: Some mothers destroy their sons without ever raising their voice.

Death by subtlety.

Death by intrusion.

Death by forced closeness.

Death by confusion.

What she did wasn't subtlety, intrusion, confusion or closeness. It was sexual abuse.

And when I finally confronted her as an adult?

Not one denial.

Not one attempt to explain.

Not one apology.

Just an immediate tactic: undermine my credibility to the extended family.

My father defended her.

My brother defended her.

Both too afraid of truth to confront it.

Both too invested in the family veneer to face reality.

Any adult who protects the abuser instead of the wounded child — even decades later — becomes part of the abuse.

They are complicit.

Trauma doesn't live in memory.

It lives in the nervous system.

And all my compulsions — the sex, the fantasy, the dopamine loops, the ego inflation — were not evidence of a defective man.

They were the survival strategies of a wounded child who never got to grow past the boundary violations he endured.

The old me didn't explode.

He starved.

And when he died, the silence that followed made room for something new to take its first breath.

My Therapist

The real catalyst who gave me the tools in understanding my subconscious and how to unpack it through shadow work was my therapist.

She understood everything— she saw what beneath the veneer. She saw the patterns, the trauma, the childhood wounds, the compulsion loops, the fear, the shame, the False Feminine, the whole architecture of collapse.

My whole life I'd been surrounded by people who either minimized my suffering or made it about them. My therapist didn't do either. She educated me. She armed me. She peeled back the layers at a pace that didn't drown me. She didn't need my story to be tidy. She didn't flinch. She taught me how to face myself without collapsing into self-hatred.

She also gave me the bedrock I'd been missing:

Christianity not as metaphysics, but as relationship.

Not as abstraction, but as narrative.

Not as perfectionism, but as salvation.

She helped me see what happened to me as a child — the betrayal, the violation, the psychological warfare — things I had buried so deep I mistook them for personality traits.

I didn't want to believe my mother could have damaged me.

But she walked me to that truth gently and firmly.

She didn't just help me heal — she helped me *understand* who I had become and why.

And once a man understands himself, he stops being controlled by the shadows he inherited.

The first flickers of clarity and hope was the moment I trusted someone with the truth — someone who could hold it without turning away.

Awakening doesn't begin with strength.

Awakening begins when you stop lying to yourself about what broke you.

Decades of pain was finally being understood instead of denied.

Something new was being born.

I knew I didn't have to go back.

Chapter Six

MECHANISM

Knock. And it Shall be Opened Unto You.

Life moves in waves. Not metaphors — *waves.*

Each one shaped by choices, by habits, by patterns, by trauma, by belief, by denial, by the things you refuse to face and the things you cling to long after they've begun killing you.

Most men don't realize they're building the wave that will eventually crash over them.

I didn't.

But looking back, I see it clearly. My wave was made of ego, compulsivity, trauma, dopamine, overachievement, silence, and fear.

Layer by layer.

Year by year.

The shape was predictable, even if the timing wasn't.

And when it finally crashed, it didn't collapse gently.

It broke with force — compression, implosion, velocity.

The kind of collapse that doesn't just knock you down.

It resets your life.

The mania of burnout isn't frenzy.

People get that wrong.

It's not chaos.

It's *momentum* — speed without direction, effort without meaning, work without soul. It's doing too much of everything for the wrong reasons.

Mania looks like:

- Overworking
- Overspending
- Overcommitting
- Overperforming
- Overpleasing
- Overindulging

It's the prefix "over" attached to everything in your life because you don't know who you actually are without all the noise.

And then, inevitably, the body, the spirit, or the mind — sometimes all three — refuse to participate anymore.

If I had to distill my burnout into one sentence, it would be this:

The path I was on could never align with my values —the values inherited from my real Father.

Not the path consulting wanted me on.

Not the path my compulsions dragged me toward.

Not the path my ego defended.

Not the path trauma carved out for me.

Not the path I thought I "should" walk.

My real Father — God — never intended for me to live and die in the misaligned life I was inhabiting. His values weren't reflected in my choices, and my soul had known it for years. Burnout wasn't a malfunction.

Burnout was a message.

A warning shot.

A shaking.

A forced confrontation.

A holy intervention.

A violent mercy.

And now we arrive at the reader — the man sitting with this chapter open, scanning these words and quietly seeing himself:

It's not your fault.

Your compulsions.

Your exhaustion.

Your shame.

Your double life.

Your dread.

Your collapse.

Your addictions.

Your emotional volatility.

Your numbness.

Your rage.

Your perfectionism.

Your porn use.

Your overeating.

Your alcohol abuse.

Your fantasy life.

Your mother wound.

Your trauma.

Your collapse of meaning...

None of that means you are defective.

You adapted.

You survived.

Your nervous system did exactly what it had to do based on the story you inherited.

You built a life on top of wounds no one helped you name.

Fine.

But now?

Now you know.

And *that's* where responsibility begins.

Because the second half of the truth is harder:

If you stay exactly as you are now, that is your fault.

If you keep getting farmed — that's your fault.

If you keep pretending your compulsions are "preferences" — that's your fault.

If you keep living a life that your soul has already rejected — your fault.

If you keep denying the wounds that shaped you — your fault.

If you keep choosing numbness over awakening — your fault.

If you keep walking the wrong path because you're afraid to disappoint someone — your fault.

Not because you're bad.

Because now you know better.

This chapter isn't meant to shame you.

It's meant to expose the trap — and then hand you the key.

Your collapse is not your identity.

Your compulsions are not your character.

Your burnout is not your destiny.

Your trauma is not your permanent story.

Your collapse is your **initiation**.

This is the moment God grabs you by the front of your shirt and says:

"We're done living the old way. Stand up. I'm not finished with you."

If you're reading this chapter and you feel something — fear, anger, hope, recognition, nausea — that's your soul responding to truth.

Good.

You're being invited into your own reconstruction.

What comes next isn't easy.

But it is possible.

In fact, it's inevitable — *if* you stop lying to yourself.

Because everything you've lost —peace, presence, clarity, strength, masculinity, purpose — you can get it back.

Burnout is not the end.

It's the beginning.

It's the moment the man you were collapses to make room for the man God intended.

This is the doorway.

Walk through it.

The Mechanical Truth

I always believed I had an anxiety problem. Or a discipline problem. Or a moral problem. The framing changed depending on the season, but the assumption never did; whatever was wrong with me lived in my thinking, my choices, my willpower, or my character.

It didn't.

What was wrong with me was mechanical.

My nervous system had been organized around one assumption since childhood: that the world was something to be defended against, managed, outperformed, or endured—but never safely inhabited. Not occasionally. Permanently.

My baseline was not calm with occasional stress.

It was stress with brief moments of calm.

That reversal is subtle. It is also devastating.

A nervous system organized around threat does not feel dramatic. It feels like readiness. It feels like competence. It feels like being the person who stays ten steps ahead so nothing goes wrong.

What it actually is—chemistry designed for emergencies running as a permanent operating condition.

Adrenaline wasn't emergency.

It was morning.

Cortisol wasn't danger.

It was baseline.

And dopamine—the chemical that normally reinforces growth, progress, and connection—had been quietly reassigned to a single job: Relief.

Relief from internal pressure that never shut off.

Once that reassignment happens, the behaviors follow automatically. Pornography. Compulsive sex. Alcohol. Sugar. Novelty. These were not moral failures.

They were a dysregulated system searching for the fastest available exit from pressure that never stopped building.

The anger at home—the rage at a light left on, a tone of voice, a sideways look—wasn't hostility.

It was overflow.

My limbic system was searching for a socially acceptable way to discharge what had accumulated.

It found one. Regularly.

The depletion I carried wasn't simple fatigue. It was a nervous system that had forgotten how to rest. Work masked it for a while—deadlines and pressure would bring adrenaline online and give me a narrow lane of functionality.

But the moment structure loosened, the flatness returned.

The only thing that reliably lifted it was fast dopamine.

Which depleted me further.

Which made the pull stronger.

The system fed itself.

My body recorded all of it long before my mind was willing to look.

A face carrying too much inflammation.

Both knees.

A disc.

Sinuses.

Food sensitivities that appeared quietly and then became unavoidable.

At the time none of it felt connected.

It was all connected.

Inflammation is what happens when stress chemistry never fully shuts off. The body absorbs the cost of a system running on overdrive—not in dramatic ways, but in slow compounding damage that one day demands a price be paid.

Sleep was the most honest measurement.

Not the origin.

The measurement.

A nervous system organized around threat does not surrender to stillness. Quiet feels unsafe. I would shift positions for hours. I would wake at three in the morning with an internal alertness that didn't match the darkness around me.

Morning would arrive already carrying dread—not because anything specific was wrong, but because my chemistry was already mobilized before the day had begun.

I was not weak.

I was not broken.

I was not defective.

I was a man living inside a regulatory system that had been quietly reprogrammed—by childhood, by trauma, by decades of high-intensity stimulation, and by an industry that understood my nervous system better than I did and farmed it accordingly.

Understanding that did not excuse anything.

But it ended the shame spiral that had been keeping me from changing anything.

A man drowning in shame about his machinery just keeps drowning.

A man who understands his machinery can actually work on it.

Nothing mystical was required to heal.

Nothing dramatic needed to fall apart.

The system simply needed to be allowed—patiently and consistently—to return to its original design.

Quiet stopped being rare.

Relief stopped being urgent.

Life became usable again.

Not louder.

Not euphoric.

Just coherent.

And that coherence changed everything.

Chapter Seven

THE WORK

The Siege

I have been here before. Days 1-7.

The first few days are never that bad.

Then the real withdrawal kicks in.

Uneasiness doesn't begin to describe it.

I can't sit still. There is an inner pressure. A burning. A deep longing. My body turns into a pressure cooker. Relief is always a screen click away — a text, a phone call, a ritual I know by heart.

Day six or seven is where it turns violent.

I am jumping in a cold plunge three times a day. I sit in the sun and listen to music just to try to calm my body. I write on my arms with a Sharpie.

"I am enough."

"Pain before peace."

"Faith under fire."

These are not affirmations. They are battle rails.

I know the pain is temporary but knowing that does not reduce it. Only commitment does.

I read scripture.

I talk to God.

But it feels less like prayer and more like Jacob wrestling in the dark. And Satan is on the other side. And I feel like I am about to be torn in two.

Any purely physical pain would be easier to bear.

This is your future self knocking at the door.

Who the fuck is going to answer?

I ask God for the ability to mirror His best qualities. I know covenants don't work — they get betrayed and forgotten. I know bargaining won't work — that's not what He wants. I know the only thing I can do is get through the day.

After the Siege

Day eight through fifteen did not feel like recovery.

They felt like **aftermath.**

Not the storm.

Not the fire.

The beach after something has already died.

They reminded me of the scene in *Lord of the Flies* — the moment when Piggy's body is found washed onto the shore.

The sky looms brooding and overcast.

Gray clouds mass like a portent.

Light filters dimly through haze.

Harsh shadows fall across a coral-strewn beach.

The sea moves gently, almost kindly, whispering solace while something final lies behind you.

That was my inner weather.

Something had ended.

Something necessary had died.

And what was coming had not yet arrived.

I was standing in the space between.

I found glimpses of peace — real ones — but they did not come with celebration. They came quietly, almost shyly, as if they were not yet sure I could be trusted with them. Moments where my breathing slowed without me forcing it. Moments where I could feel warmth instead of pressure. Moments where my body didn't feel like it was about to tear itself apart.

And still — the clouds remained.

They kept me aware that this was not finished. That what was emerging was fragile. That what had been stripped away had not yet been replaced. That I was still inside a crossing, not at the other side of it.

I was no longer being chased by the fire.

But I was not yet living in sunlight.

I walked.

I sat.

I prayed.

Not dramatic prayers.

Quiet ones.

Honest ones.

Simple ones like:

Keep me steady.

Help me stay.

Let what is dying finish dying.

Let what is being born survive.

This was the first place where peace showed up — not as comfort, not as reward, but as a thin band of light slipping through a heavy sky.

Enough to keep going.

Not enough to let me forget where I was.

And I didn't want to forget.

Because this shoreline mattered.

The fork did not become visible because I suddenly grew stronger.

It became visible because my body was finally shown what peace felt like.

Day thirteen.

A warm, cloudy, rainy evening in Columbus. Soft gray light — the kind that quiets everything. After my workout, sauna, and a brief cold plunge, I took Benjamin for a walk. A warm breeze drifted up from the southwest. A few raindrops touched my face — not enough to send me back inside, just enough to remind me that I was alive.

No invisible hum of anxiety underneath everything.

Just presence — pure, unguarded, wordless peace.

That sentence marked the end of a life.

I realized in that quiet moment that this feeling was priceless. No amount of money, achievement, or attention could ever match it. I had spent years chasing stimulation — news feeds, validation, desire, noise — anything to distract me from the pain of stillness. That night, there was no chase.

Only being.

The warm rain.

The rhythm of Benjamin's steps beside me.

The soft wind moving through the trees.

Grace — not as an idea, but as an experience in the body.

That was the first proof that a different life was not theoretical.

It was livable.

I knew there was more work ahead. I knew healing was not a straight line. But I had finally felt what I had been fighting for: the simple holiness of being present, whole, and free.

From that evening forward, the two roads were no longer equal.

One road promised relief.

The other promised peace.

And my body had already chosen.

The Gray Corridor

By the time Day 23 arrived, the war inside my body was no longer loud, but something equally unsettling had taken its place. I felt disoriented and unsure of who I was, not in an abstract or philosophical way, but in a bodily one. It felt as though the structure that had held me together for decades had loosened, and I was still learning what shape I was going to take without it.

I wrote that it felt like dissolving, similar to a psilocybin trip.

What I was standing inside during this phase was not "recovery." It was identity thinning.

And the only other time in my life I had ever felt that particular kind of thinning — the erasure of narrative self — came from a very different and very unsuccessful attempt to shortcut this process.

Several years earlier, during a failed recovery run, I tried to use neuroplasticity as a reset button. I microdosed psilocybin for weeks, hoping it would soften old grooves and make change easier. Instead, it made my compulsions worse. So I escalated.

3.78 grams of Cubensis B+.

In a ginger-steeped tea.

Twenty minutes later, my body collapsed into a heavy internal buzzing. My head vibrated. My limbs weakened so badly I had to lie down. Multi-colored, highly detailed, high-resolution patterns filled my vision. The floor began to undulate. Carbon-like tubes appeared in my visual field. I felt the presence of something dark and unclean.

Outside, the stark white stalks of milkweed glowed against a winter sky that felt hostile. Even squirrels looked like thieves.

And then my identity disappeared.

My identity as Tony Crandall — my history, my perception of myself, my life story, my trajectory as I knew it — was gone.

Not frightening.

Just erased.

No past.

No future.

Just blank existence.

Later that afternoon I threw up on myself in the bathtub. I walked into my vanity and threw out all my weed, all my Xanax, every prescription bottle I owned — and I never looked back.

And it still did not work.

The compulsions quieted for a few weeks and then returned.

Because what I had touched chemically, I had not metabolized.

I had experienced ego death — but not self-rebuilding.

That is why the Gray Corridor felt familiar to my body.

Not because I was slipping backward —but because I was finally crossing the same interior territory sober, slow, and permanent.

Shrooms. Ibogaine. Ketamine.

From my experience — shortcuts are bullshit.

You have to do the work.

The old internal voice that used to narrate everything had gone quiet, and nothing had yet replaced it. The familiar tension that once kept me braced was no longer there, but neither was the sense of momentum that had driven my life for years. I was standing inside a long, flat interior space with no clear markers to tell me who I was becoming.

What rose in the absence of stimulation surprised me. I did not crave fantasy, novelty, or lust. I craved real human connection. I wanted warmth, closeness, and presence. I wanted to hold someone and be held, not sexually and not for stimulation, but for safety. I wanted the simple experience of sitting near another human being without having to perform, escape, or prove anything.

My body reflected that shift. My limbs felt heavy. My energy stayed low. There were days when flu-like sensations passed through me, and my body seemed to want warmth more than anything else, sauna heat, blankets, quiet rooms, and simple food that felt like care rather than fuel. Grilled cheese and bananas became grounding in a way protein shakes never had. Sleep was uneven, but I could feel my system trying to recalibrate itself in real time.

At the same time, something quiet and astonishing was unfolding beneath the surface. I began noticing that I was starting to care about women as people rather than as objects of stimulation. Attraction slowed down. It felt calmer, more respectful, and no longer chemically frantic. It was not dramatic. It was simply honest. In my journal I wrote, "My value is coming online." That sentence marked the beginning of self-respect replacing self-betrayal.

Day 24 carried a different quality. I woke with clarity and permanently closed the door on the manipulative patterns I had once been entangled in—not through anger, but through sober understanding. For years I had used anger to propel myself away from what hurt me. That day, I did not need anger. Truth was enough. Clarity without hate became my new form of freedom.

I painted trim in the kitchen, threw a frisbee for Benjamin, listened to my son play guitar upstairs, and felt peace in those ordinary moments. The presence I experienced did not feel like discipline. It felt like grounded discernment. James 1:2–4 lingered in the background of my day, not as a verse to perform, but as a lived truth—steadfastness forming through quiet endurance. "Consider it pure joy, my brothers and sisters, whenever you face trials of many kinds, because you know that the testing of your faith produces perseverance. Let perseverance finish its work so that you may be mature and complete, not lacking anything."

Day 25 arrived my first uninterrupted night of sleep since that camping out in Yosemite. I woke calm and clear, without the familiar static running through my body. Coffee barely registered as a stimulant anymore. I drank half and forgot the rest. This was not willpower; it was chemistry catching up with peace. Regulation was returning.

With that regulation came a different kind of challenge. Guilt surfaced—not as conscience, but as an awareness of past manipulation and harm. I did not excuse it, and I did not reopen old relational doors. I simply acknowledged it and stayed oriented forward. I realized that I loved myself more than I loved fake attention. That realization marked a milestone: self-preservation replacing self-betrayal.

In the quiet that followed, something deeper opened. Reflections on my father surfaced—not with resentment, but with clarity. I saw how fear, shame, and passivity had shaped him, and how those grooves had shaped me. What once felt like contamination now felt like context. I recognized how my drive to teach my sons courage and confidence was born from a boy who never wanted them to feel as powerless as he once had. I no longer needed to overcorrect. Strength was becoming steady rather than reactive.

By Day 28, the corridor flattened into what I could only describe as doldrums. I woke frustrated that this phase lacked the epic struggle of the early weeks. "No wind... my boat just sits here," I wrote. Emotion was muted, energy moderate, and faith dry but disciplined. Libido flickered, not as a threat but as a sign of slow restoration. I felt the pull of temptation briefly and chose a sauna, yogurt, and quiet instead of testing myself. The sentence that captured that day was simple and decisive: "I wanted to, but I want my recovery more."

This stretch was not glamorous. It was humbling. It required the discipline of being rather than performing, enduring rather than dramatizing, and trusting a process that did not provide fireworks or applause. I was not trying to return to a former version of myself. I was allowing something new to assemble, slowly and quietly, from clarity rather than nostalgia.

This was the Gray Corridor.

Not empty.

Not punishment.

Sacred, slow, and necessary.

The Quiet Crossing

The next phase did not arrive with fireworks.

The war was no longer loud — but the victory had not yet learned how to speak.

I woke restless, unimpressed, still impatient with how unremarkable this felt.

There was no chaos.

There was no collapse.

There was just stillness — and the strange discipline of staying inside it.

That was new.

Quiet began training a different muscle.

The ability to remain present without stimulation.

The ability to endure neutral days without manufacturing drama.

The ability to let the nervous system complete work that could not be rushed.

I stopped looking for noise that would make me feel something.

Reddit went dark.

Distraction stopped negotiating.

I wasn't returning to an old version of myself.

There was no "again." There was only "becoming."

By the early thirties, something inside me began to stabilize in a way I had not felt in decades.

Sleep deepened.

Breath slowed.

Emotion stopped surging.

My body began revealing itself — not in strength or performance, but in **calm.**

I stopped bargaining with my life.

I stopped waiting for permission to be whole.

Integrity became my new stimulant.

Truth became my new safety.

Virtual ties fell away without drama.

"If you're not face-to-face with somebody, you don't know them."

Peace stopped feeling like a mood and started behaving like a structure.

This was the crossing.

Not a finish line.

A handoff.

The old operating self still spoke —but it no longer held veto power.

I wasn't managing urges anymore.

I was governed by something quieter.

Something steadier.

Something that didn't need exits.

And once that authority transferred, it did not come back.

Chapter Eight

THE QUIET BASELINE

There is a moment when recovery ends, not because the work is finished, but because the body is no longer living inside threat.

It does not arrive as a victory and it does not feel like relief. Days 30-60 brought no sense of completion, no emotional release, and no internal celebration. It arrives quietly, as a change in orientation. The world no longer feels like a place that must be managed, negotiated, or outperformed. It simply feels present.

I first noticed it the morning after I arrived in Tallahassee.

I offloaded my RT from the trailer under the moss hanging from the live oaks, the air was warm and still, the sky wide and untroubled. On every ride before that one, no matter how far I had traveled or how much freedom I thought I was chasing, I had arrived armored and internally braced, carrying a low-grade readiness for pressure that never fully left my system. Even joy had always been filtered through that posture.

That morning, it was gone.

I was relaxed in a way that had nothing to do with ease and nothing to do with excitement. I was simply present. There was no inner narration, no checking for danger, no rehearsal of what might be required of me next. I was not proving readiness to anything. I was standing in the world without resistance, and nothing inside me was arguing with the fact that I was there.

I did not name it in the moment. I did not mark it as a milestone. I only noticed that the noise that had always occupied the background of my days was no longer running.

The ride that followed felt different because my movements were no longer being shaped by tension. They were being shaped by presence. I was not riding to outrun anything. I was riding because I was there.

That was the first proof.

The Panhandle ride had not been an escape and it had not been a reward. It had been a planned interruption. I had spent more than forty days inside a closed recovery arc, living in a narrowed geography, working quietly through physiological and psychological recalibration, and I could feel the edges of my world starting to contract. The trip was chosen deliberately as a way to widen the lens again, to remind my system that life still existed beyond discipline and routine, and to reintroduce movement without urgency.

In the past, movement had always carried a charge. My riding history was built around speed, technical aggression, and environments that rewarded vigilance. Roads like the Triple Nickel, the Dragon, Beartooth Pass, the Pig Trail, the Cherohala Skyway, and the Moonshiner 28 had trained my body to associate motorcycles with intensity, edge, and controlled risk. I had learned to armor myself before rides not out of fear, but out of conditioning. Even pleasure had required access friction and readiness.

That posture had become automatic. It had followed me into every version of freedom I thought I was choosing.

Tallahassee did not activate it.

The ride did not feel like a release from pressure. It felt like an expression of calm that had already settled inside me. The roads were wide, the light was open, the air was still, and nothing in my system rose to meet the day as if it were a contest. I was not trying to extract anything from the ride. I was not testing limits or proving resilience. I was simply moving through space without resistance.

The days along the Panhandle began to register differently.

Not as highlights.

Not as escapes.

As presence.

On St. James Island, an eagle stood in the shallows eating a fish with the casual focus of a man working through a bagel. There was nothing cinematic about it. It did not feel symbolic in the moment. It simply felt real, and I noticed that reality no longer required commentary.

In Apalachicola, a fried grouper sandwich and an IPA tasted right. Not indulgent. Not compensatory. Just finished. The food did not feel like reward. It felt like nourishment returning to its place in ordinary life.

The Orange Beach Fairfield Inn hot tub steamed under still air. The water was suspiciously calm, the cleanliness unconfirmed, and somehow none of that mattered. I did not need perfection to feel settled. I only needed to be there.

On a quiet stretch of roadside wildflowers, monarch butterflies moved through in the middle of their long migration. I stood and watched without urgency. They were not performing. They were continuing. I recognized the motion without turning it into meaning.

Later, on Route 20, the air changed. Pine resin drifted through open miles under mid-seventies sun, and the scent did not trigger memory. It registered as sensation. Clean. Present. Immediate.

Colors felt fuller. Sounds carried weight. Taste did not need enhancement. Smell did not require interpretation. Nothing felt filtered through effort, vigilance, or anticipation.

The world was not louder.

It was clearer.

This was what presence meant. Not awareness. Not gratitude. But life arriving without compression.

The filter was gone.

And the body knew it before the mind ever tried to explain it.

Normal without Collapse

Around day 50, the quiet that arrived in Florida did not disappear when I came home.

But my body did.

On the drive north, I could feel it starting. The familiar scratch in my throat. The heaviness that sits just behind the sternum when something deeper is waking up. I had planned to stop and see a friend on the way back, but I did not. I could already feel my system moving into repair.

It did not feel like a simple cold. It lingered. It dragged. It settled in and stayed.

I lost ground.

Cold plunges fell away first. Then workouts. Then sauna. Parts of my diet followed. My physical pillars thinned out, and with them my margin for friction. My system became more vulnerable. Triggers were harder to manage. Energy narrowed. I lapsed a few times.

But the loop did not take me.

That is the difference.

In the past, losing structure had meant losing altitude. A disruption like this would have turned into a spiral. This time, it did not. Even while sick, even while stripped of many of the physical anchors I had relied on, the core held.

Thanksgiving arrived inside that weakened stretch.

In earlier years, it had always been a high-stress performance. Cooking had been pressure. Navigation of shared space had been a trigger. Other people's urgency would bleed into my system and tighten it from the inside. Holidays had felt commercial, exhausting, and strangely adversarial.

This year was different.

I felt present.

Not guarded.

Not braced.

Just present.

I could feel a trigger rising before it fully formed, and instead of reacting to it, I simply stayed with it. I told myself to remain present. To breathe. To let the chemical echo move through. It did. The surge passed inside ten minutes. Then it passed again. And again.

It was the calmest Thanksgiving I can remember.

Not special.

Not emotional.

Just human.

This is where the truth of healing becomes visible.

Healing is not linear.

There are stretches where the nervous system is under heavier demand, and the body enters deep recalibration. During these phases, immunity runs lower. Energy narrows. Old supports fall away temporarily. The system becomes more sensitive, more easily fatigued, more vulnerable to illness.

The sickness feels heavier because the body is no longer masking repair with adrenaline. It lasts longer because resources are being redirected into rewiring rather than performance. The system is not weak. It is busy.

This is the middle ground that most people misread.

You are not failing.

You are not sliding backward.

You are temporarily exposed while new structure is being laid down.

And by this stage of recovery, something crucial has already changed.

Even when the pillars thin.

Even when the body is tired.

Even when routines fall apart.

The loop does not own you anymore.

You are not falling.

You are being rebuilt.

And you have enough inside you now to stay upright while it happens.

The Season Without a Name

Days 90 through 120 did not feel heroic.

They felt exposed.

The acute cravings were gone. The gray corridor had thinned. I was no longer fighting daily siege warfare inside my own mind. The pillars held most days—cold plunge, lifting, protein, Scripture, structure. When I drifted from them, I could feel the edges soften, but I did not collapse.

I slipped a few times.

That sentence used to carry devastation. Now it carried contrast.

I did not spiral. I did not disappear into shame. I did not build a narrative of failure. Sometimes I deferred an urge and walked away. Sometimes I chose poorly but did not repeat it the next day. Weakness remained possible. Captivity did not.

That should have felt like triumph.

It didn't.

It felt like something else was being dismantled.

There was a moment during that stretch when I saw myself clearly in a way I hadn't before.

Not abstractly. Not as a theological concept. Not as trauma analysis.

Clearly.

The false flattery. The subtle positioning. The boundary pushing disguised as curiosity. The attention extraction dressed up as connection.

I could feel it in my stomach.

It made me sick.

I could see how transparent it must have been. How people could probably smell it long before I did. The need beneath it. The hunger for significance. The quiet attempt to pull validation from wherever it was available.

And the uncomfortable truth was this: given my wiring, my history, my vigilance, my unmet needs—there is no version of me in those years who would have behaved differently.

That did not require forgiveness.

It required growth.

The sickness did not turn into shame. It turned into respect.

Respect for the boy who learned to survive by extracting attention. Respect for the man who had mistaken that extraction for connection. Respect for the simple mechanics of cause and effect.

If I had been operating from hunger, so were others. If I could engineer connection without realizing it, so could they.

The awareness softened me.

Not sentimentally.

Soberly.

At the same time, something else was dissolving.

After viewing God as an abstraction growing up in a Christian Science household, over the past several years as I started my independent study of the Bible, I had related to God as though He were more a divine version of a true Father figure. I loved Him the way a wounded child loves a rescuer—emotionally, sentimentally, sometimes desperately. There was comfort in that. There was warmth.

That warmth began to thin.

What remained felt clearer and less familiar.

God as Life itself.

Not anthropomorphic. Not an English-speaking presence who affirmed me in human language. Not a cosmic therapist. Not an emotional co-regulator.

Life.

The structure of reality. The source of breath. The force that animates and withdraws. The designer and creator of all. The One that gives us this gift of living in the tension between good and evil. The free will to overcome our human nature and do good things. To have wisdom, courage, loyalty. To chose the difficult, but right path.

That shift did not frighten me.

It clarified me.

But it stripped away comfort.

God seemed less tied to a religious point of view.

My faith grew quieter. Less theatrical. Less emotionally charged. I found myself irritated by passages of Scripture that once stirred me. The Old Testament felt repetitive. My morning reading felt disciplined rather than sentimental.

Repentance no longer felt like pleading.

It felt like calibration.

I was no longer climbing toward righteousness as though it were distant. I was attempting to align with what had already been granted.

And I knew this relationship was not finished. If anything, it was just beginning in a more honest way. I now had enough mental space to unwind it further—without panic, without bargaining.

The softness left.

Clarity remained.

Without attention extraction and without sentimental spirituality, something quiet filled the space.

Silence.

There had always been a perpetual distracting undercurrent of vigilance, urgency, internal argument, rehearsed conversations... tension. Even my vices had momentum. Even my anger had shape.

This layer was gone.

And nothing replaced it.

I did not feel like myself.

That unsettled me more than temptation ever had.

Who was I if I wasn't braced? Who was I if I wasn't striving? Who was I if I wasn't engineering significance or negotiating divine reassurance?

There were days I missed the intensity.

There were days the quiet felt like emptiness.

But the quiet did not collapse me.

My body continued changing without announcement.

I began waking up hungry.

Sleep deepened. I slept longer without the restless midnight surges that had defined me for decades. Dreams returned with texture and narrative.

I noticed something small and strange: I used to over-chew my food, sometimes forcing myself to swallow. As if bracing even in digestion. I swallowed more naturally, without tension.

It was as though my body no longer expected threat.

The change was not dramatic.

It was steady.

I closed loops.

Around Day 99, I installed a humidifier and solenoid that had sat in a closet for three years. I replaced a dimmer switch with a standard one so airflow in the house would stabilize—finally letting the Big Ass Fan in my two-story living room do what it was designed to do. I placed hygrometers throughout the rooms and began measuring humidity instead of guessing. The task itself was trivial.

The act was not.

For years I lived in doing big projects around the house- the deck, laundry room, renovating the bathrooms. But deferred smaller seeming less significant maintenance—ambient friction, half-finished ideas, small acts postponed indefinitely. My mind mirrored that environment: constant partial attention, scrolling, postponement, quiet leakage of agency.

Installing that switch felt like sealing a circuit.

Not optimization.

Hygiene.

The old model of my life constricted flow in subtle ways. It didn't destroy me outright. It siphoned attention and momentum until pressure built.

Now I was restoring flow.

Quietly.

I felt weighted. Like I was holding something of substance. Like I could wield it to its best effect.

Discipline, intellect, faith, physical training, restraint—these qualities had always existed in me. But they had operated independently. Under pressure they fragmented.

Now they were beginning to move together.

I didn't have language for it at the time.

I only knew I could feel something in my spine that wasn't aggression, wasn't dominance, wasn't urgency.

Substance.

I did not yet know who I was becoming.

But I could feel that I was no longer fragmented.

And I could feel that whatever was forming had weight.

When I boarded the flight for New Zealand, I was not escaping.

I was carrying something.

Expansion

The rain between Franz Josef and Hokitika on South Island was not cinematic.

It was blinding.

Torrential sheets came sideways across the road. My visor fogged almost immediately. My rain gloves soaked through. The temperature dropped just enough to stiffen my fingers. My rain suit saved me from hypothermia, but I could barely see beyond the taillight in front of me before it disappeared into gray.

At 80 kilometers per hour in those conditions, there is no room for abstraction.

You keep it between the lines.

You watch the camber.

You read the shine of the asphalt.

You modulate throttle.

You stay upright.

I cracked the visor despite the rain. The sting of cold drops hit my face like needles. It was the only way to see. Breath escaped in small bursts to attempt to lessen fogging. Every sense narrowed to the next thirty meters of road.

There was no soundtrack.

No reflection.

No metaphor forming in my head.

Only presence.

The old version of me would have layered meaning onto it. Would have imagined telling the story later. Would have framed the difficulty as conquest.

There was none of that.

Just the work of staying upright.

I am alive in the moment.

When the rain began to thin, it did not stop all at once. It softened in waves. The road lightened. The fog on my visor retreated. I lifted the face shield fully for the first time in an hour.

The sting was gone.

In its place were shades of purple and gray I cannot fully describe. Dense clouds rising out of the forest as if the land itself were breathing. Mist lifting off treetops in slow spirals. Wet asphalt reflecting the sky like brushed metal.

It was stunning.

And I did not reach for it.

I did not imagine sharing it.

I did not narrate it.

I did not try to capture it beyond a photograph or two.

There was only presence.

And gratitude.

The gratitude was not emotional. It was not swelling or dramatic. It was simple acknowledgment.

I am here.

I can see this.

I am upright.

I am steady.

The feeling of ballast that I had in the weeks prior did not disappear in New Zealand.

It traveled with me.

Throughout the trip, that pattern repeated.

Beauty without grasping.

Silence without loneliness.

Motion without urgency.

I rode through valleys where the road bent like a ribbon thrown across green hills. I stood at overlooks where the wind pressed against my jacket and the horizon stretched in quiet indifference. I drank coffee alone without rehearsing imaginary conversations.

There was no internal argument running beneath it.

No hunger to extract significance from strangers.

No need to be seen.

That absence was more striking than the scenery.

I was not performing for anyone.

Not even for myself.

New Zealand did not change me.

It revealed whether I had changed.

In torrential rain, I stayed steady.

In beauty, I did not grasp.

In solitude, I did not project.

In discomfort, I did not resent.

That was new.

But I did not name it then.

I only rode.

When I boarded the flight home, I was not returning to a battleground.

I was returning with something.

I did not know how it would hold under proximity, under history, under conversation.

But I could feel its weight.

Return

The house did not look different when I walked back in.

The floors were the same.

The walls were the same.

The routines were the same.

But something in me was not.

The conversations that followed were not dramatic. No ultimatums. No emotional outbursts. No grand reconciliations.

Just discussion.

For years, discussions in that house had carried voltage. Even silence felt like negotiation. My body would brace before words were fully formed. I would prepare arguments internally before the other person finished speaking.

This time, I sat.

And listened.

Not to prepare a response.

Not to position.

Not to win.

Not to withdraw.

Just to hear.

At some point during those conversations, I noticed something.

I was at ease.

No surge of adrenaline.

No rehearsed counterpoint forming beneath the surface.

And most surprising of all—I was just present.

That realization did not occur in the moment.

It surfaced afterward.

I replayed the conversation in my mind and searched for the old signals— the calculation, the subtle aggression.

They were not there.

For fifteen years, proximity had activated defense.

Now it did not.

That was the proof.

Not the ride.

Not the rain.

Not the weight.

This.

Relational regulation under historic trigger.

I was not trying to preserve something.

I was not trying to destroy something.

I was not trying to control something.

Act III is not an escape.

It is forward motion.

Not toward conquest.

Not toward reinvention.

Forward without armor.

I do not know precisely what it will hold.

I do know this: I do not fear the final outcome.

Chapter Nine

RECKONING AND THE SEVEN TENETS

Up to this point, I have told the story chronologically — the trauma, the compulsive loops, the physical regulation, the daily grind, the motorcycle rides, the gradual stabilization. But narrative alone does not explain what actually happened inside me. To understand that we have to revisit those same days through a different lens.

What I experienced was not simply behavioral recovery. It was structural reorganization. And the cleanest psychological map I have encountered for understanding that reorganization comes from Carl Jung.

What follows is not theory for its own sake. It is an attempt to explain, in plain terms, what was happening beneath the surface while I was cold plunging, walking the dog, lifting weights, and forcing myself to stay present. The behaviors were visible. The architecture underneath them was not.

To understand the arc fully, we have to look at the interior.

Let's start back at "stuck."

It was a perfect May morning.

I had just cooked breakfast and carried the plate out to the deck. Benjamin — my chocolate lab, my best friend — sat at my feet. I opened the slats on the pergola and let air and sunlight filter through in narrow bands. The grass was turning lush green. The red oaks were coming alive again. My beloved bluebirds were raising their first clutch without harassment — at least for now — from the house sparrows.

My favorite time of year.

I was sitting on the deck I built with my own hands. Every board measured. Every screw driven. Everything around that which I had tended, shaped, and protected. These things answered me when I asked anything at all of them. The trees responded to pruning. The birds responded to protection. The dog responded to care.

And yet what should have been blue, green, and gold registered as gray.

Not dramatic despair. A flattening.

No clients calling. No outside urgency. No fire to put out. For years urgency had organized me. Pressure had given me direction. Without it, there was no pull forward. Nothing pushing. Nothing drawing me.

Only stillness.

And beneath the stillness, agitation.

Childhood trauma. The insecure overachiever persona. The compulsive loops meant to soothe itinerant pain slowly becoming a prison. Not just a prison for my body.

A prison for my soul.

I couldn't go forward like this.

I am not going to die like this.

I am stuck.

How the fuck do I lever this loose and become the person I am supposed to be? A man my kids could learn from. A man they could be proud of. A man who, after he is gone, is remembered well.

But deeper than that:

How do I play the cards my Father dealt me in the best possible way?

How do I honor Him?

How do I honor myself?

How do I honor the animals that gave their lives to feed me this morning?

I am stuck.

But what does that actually mean?

If I can define it, I can move it.

I have walked into complex systems and untangled them for a living. I can do the same here. I can apply that same logic inward. No more vague language. No more self-pity. Define the constraint. Identify the distortion. Rebuild the structure.

I had just read James Hollis' work synthesizing Jung's teaching on individuation. One line kept ringing in my head:

"The privilege of a lifetime is to become who you truly are."

That line would not leave me.

"What you resist does not disappear. It grows."

I needed purpose. I needed meaning. But I was sitting there with a fried dopamine circuit and a life organized around urgency and relief.

I wrote seven principles distilled from Hollis' work. Not goals. Not productivity hacks. Guiding principles. Things I would hold close to me if I was going to move at all, as the tenets that would guide my recovery.

The Seven Tenets:

1. Embrace the stillness. Turn off the noise.

2. Reconnect with curiosity. The freedom to find a spark.

3. Engage in active reflection. What is this feeling trying to teach me?

4. Find meaning, not happiness. What hard thing am I willing to do because it matters?

5. Seek soulful nourishment. Things that don't ignite your brain's pleasure center but awaken your soul.

6. Surround yourself with depth. Books. People. Ideas that stir your soul. Conversations that feel like mining. People who challenge you to grow.

7. Let go of the timeline. There is no quick fix. Clarity does not always emerge at first. What emerges is always worth the wait. Stop trying to go back.

I didn't know where this would take me.

I didn't know how hard it would be.

I didn't know what it would cost.

But I knew there were no other alternatives.

That morning was not dramatic. No one saw it. No one applauded it.

But something in me shifted from drift to decision.

And once that shift happened, the rest became inevitable.

I did not need inspiration. I needed a map.

I learned that I had mistaken intensity for transformation. I believed that if I could decide harder, focus longer, discipline more ruthlessly, I could overpower whatever defect trailed me. Effort had always worked professionally. Why wouldn't it work internally?

Because effort operates inside a structure.

And if the structure itself is distorted, more effort simply reinforces the distortion.

When I encountered Jung seriously — first through James Hollis, then through Jung's own writing — something in me did not feel inspired. It felt exposed. As if someone had quietly diagrammed the interior mechanics I had been living inside without language.

Jung did not reduce the human being to behavior, nor to morality, nor to trauma alone. He described a layered interior architecture.

Consciousness is only a narrow band of awareness. It is the part of us that narrates our life, claims identity, sets goals, evaluates right and wrong, chooses words. It feels sovereign because it is what we can see.

But it is not sovereign.

The **ego** is the organizing center of that conscious field. It constructs coherence. It builds persona. It negotiates social survival. It defends against humiliation. It selects which traits to display and which to suppress. It maintains the story of who we think we are.

The ego is not evil. It is necessary. It keeps a child attached. It keeps a teenager adaptive. It keeps an adult functioning.

But the ego is an executive, not a king.

Beyond the thin strip of consciousness lies the vast **unconscious** — not mystical fog, but accumulated imprint. Early attachment patterns. Trauma responses. Suppressed emotion. Instinctual drives. Unmet needs. Grief. Aggression. Sexuality. Creativity. Shame. Longing. Fear. Strength that frightened authority. Vulnerability that threatened survival.

The unconscious does not argue. It influences.

It shapes mood.

It steers attraction.

It triggers reaction.

It produces dreams.

It leaks through the body.

It insists through compulsion.

Within that unconscious sits what Jung called the **shadow** — the disowned portions of the personality. Not simply "darkness," but everything the ego could not integrate without jeopardizing attachment, status, safety, or moral self-image.

A boy who learns that need invites rejection buries need.

A child who discovers that anger threatens attachment buries anger.

A teenager who finds that vulnerability invites ridicule buries vulnerability.

A young man who equates worth with performance buries weakness.

The ego survives by narrowing.

But nothing buried disappears.

What is rejected does not dissolve. It waits. It gathers pressure. And when the ego refuses integration, the shadow does not become quiet. It becomes indirect.

It acts out.

It seeks discharge.

It surfaces in distorted forms.

That was not abstract psychology for me. It was autobiography.

My vigilant nervous system built an overachieving persona. Competence became armor. Achievement became identity. Performance became moral cover. I became disciplined, responsible, rational — the man who could be trusted in complex systems.

But beneath that persona, the shadow held what could not be shown: hunger for affirmation, loneliness that felt adolescent, grief that never metabolized, rage at powerlessness, desire that contradicted moral narrative, exhaustion from decades of vigilance.

When my nervous system remained chronically mobilized, dopamine lost its original function. It stopped reinforcing growth and began reinforcing relief. Compulsion was not rebellion. It was shadow pressure seeking temporary quiet inside a dysregulated organism.

I was not uniquely corrupt.

I was structurally fragmented.

And then Jung named something even more destabilizing: the **Self**.

Not the ego-self that introduces itself in a boardroom. Not the persona. The Self, capital S, is the organizing center of the entire psyche — conscious and unconscious together. It is the blueprint of psychological wholeness. It exerts a gravitational pull across a lifetime, drawing a person toward integration whether the ego cooperates or not.

Individuation, in Jung's language, is the lifelong process by which the ego gradually relinquishes its illusion of total control and enters into right relationship with the deeper totality of the psyche.

It is not self-improvement.

It is self-integration.

When I looked back over the siege, the gray corridor, the pillars, the rides, the relational steadiness, something shifted. I had interpreted those months as recovery from addiction. Through this lens, they were early-stage individuation. The ego was losing its monopoly. The shadow was surfacing without overwhelming the system. The Self was reorganizing the interior.

But Jung stops at psychological totality.

Scripture completes the orientation.

The Self, as Jung describes it, pulls toward wholeness. But wholeness, by itself, is not a moral category. A person can be psychologically integrated and still self-referential. Integration without vertical alignment can become refined narcissism — coherent, powerful, and unmoored.

For me, the **soul** is not merely psychological totality. It is the dimension of the human being oriented toward God — accountable to something higher than preference, comfort, or coherence. If the Self organizes the psyche horizontally, the soul anchors it vertically. The Self integrates the personality; the soul submits it.

Without individuation, religion becomes repression. The ego attempts righteousness while the shadow festers underground. That tension produces hypocrisy, projection, and private contradiction.

Without vertical orientation, individuation becomes aesthetic. The person becomes integrated but self-justifying. Meaning collapses into self-expression.

Together, they form a hierarchy.

Ego disciplined under Self.

Self aligned under God.

That hierarchy is not diminishment. It is stabilization.

When I began to understand this structure, self-hatred lost its grip. I could see that I had reacted as a threat-conditioned, high-functioning human male would predictably react under prolonged internal pressure. My adaptations were not exotic evil. They were incomplete integration.

This shift did not absolve me.

It did something more important.

It removed self-contempt from the process.

And without self-contempt, responsibility becomes possible. Without shame as identity, growth becomes sustainable.

I stopped calling adaptation evil.

I began calling it unfinished.

When I re-read the first 120 days through this lens, the language shifts.

What I had called recovery was something more specific.

It was the ego losing its monopoly.

The siege was not just withdrawal. It was ego panic.

Day six or seven — when my body felt like a pressure cooker and relief was one click away — that was not simply craving. That was shadow energy rising without its usual anesthetic. Hunger. Loneliness. Sexual charge. Rage. All of it stripped of outlet. The ego had spent decades managing those forces indirectly. Now it had removed the sedative and was face to face with what it had buried.

Cold plunge three times a day was not biohacking.

It was containment.

Writing on my arms — "I am enough. Pain before peace. Faith under fire." — was not affirmation culture. It was ego discipline under pressure from the unconscious. The shadow wanted discharge. The ego wanted relief. Something deeper was asking for endurance.

The Seven Tenets were important in navigating that space.

They were not habits. They were orientation commitments. They were the ego's first act of humility — a decision to submit to a direction larger than comfort.

But the Tenets did not heal me.

The Pillars did something different.

When I began stabilizing protein intake, lifting with consistency, cold plunging, regulating sleep, anchoring mornings in Scripture, and setting hard relational boundaries, something biological shifted. Cortisol quieted. Dopamine spikes softened. My prefrontal cortex stopped losing ground to limbic urgency.

The Pillars were not moral.

They were regulatory.

They lowered the internal noise enough that shadow could surface without detonating the system.

Then came the Gray Corridor.

Weeks four and five.

The absence of stimulation.

The flatness.

The cream-of-wheat neutrality.

The sense that I was only half alive.

At the time, it felt like loss.

Through this lens, it was ego dethronement.

For decades my ego had been fueled by intensity — achievement, stimulation, urgency, validation. When those fuels were withdrawn, nothing rushed in to replace them. I was meeting myself without persona charge.

The psilocybin memory from years earlier suddenly made sense in a different way. Back then, I had chemically dissolved ego boundaries for a few hours. It felt like annihilation because the system was unregulated. In the Gray Corridor, ego thinning happened slowly and soberly. Identity softened. Narrative quieted. The old internal voice that insisted on significance lost volume.

That was not depression.

It was reorganization.

Day thirteen — walking in warm rain with Benjamin, jaw unclenched, chest open, no hum beneath the moment — that was not simply peace.

That was Self beginning to organize experience without ego interference.

I was not extracting meaning from the walk.

I was not narrating it.

I was not rehearsing future conversations.

Presence replaced performance.

On Day twenty-four, painting trim in the kitchen and listening to my son play guitar upstairs, I felt grounded rather than restless. That was shadow integration in miniature. The hunger for stimulation was not gone. It was simply no longer in charge.

Thanksgiving that year revealed something even more telling.

For fifteen years, proximity in my own house had activated vigilance. Tone shifts felt like threat. Silence felt like negotiation. My shoulders would rise before words formed. I would prepare rebuttals in advance.

That Thanksgiving, triggers rose and passed within minutes. I felt them in my body — the tightening, the chemical surge — and then they dissipated without escalation. That was not self-control. That was ego under new governance.

Projection had weakened.

In New Zealand, riding through blinding rain between Franz Josef and Hokitika, cracking the visor to keep from fogging, focusing only on the next thirty meters of asphalt — that was not adrenaline seeking. It was regulated presence under demand. The old version of me would have layered metaphor over the experience in real time. This time, there was no internal narrator trying to extract meaning.

In the clear stretch that followed — purple and gray clouds lifting off wet forest, mist rising, the road reflecting the sky — I did not grasp at the beauty. I did not imagine sharing it. I did not convert it into identity.

That absence was the point.

Shadow desire was no longer hijacking awe.

Relational steadiness after returning home was perhaps the clearest marker. Sitting in conversation without bracing. Listening without calculating outcome. Not fearing the final result. That was ego relinquishing defensive dominance.

And beneath all of it, something else had shifted quietly.

My faith had moved from emotional dependency to structural alignment.

Earlier in my life, I had loved God sentimentally — as rescuer, as comforter, as affirmation. In those 120 days, that warmth thinned and something steadier replaced it.

That shift felt clarifying.

The Self organizing the psyche horizontally.

The soul orienting it vertically.

Ego no longer trying to be sovereign.

Self no longer competing with faith.

Faith no longer suppressing shadow.

Shadow no longer leaking through compulsion.

What had once been a civil war became hierarchy.

I was not healed in 120 days.

I was stabilized.

The ego had loosened.

The shadow had surfaced without destroying me.

The Self had begun organizing experience.

The soul had re-anchored under God.

This was not transformation.

It was the beginning of integration.

I still have days when my nervous system is too reactive.

Days when agitation rises for no obvious reason. When the old currents flicker. When doubt whispers that none of this mattered.

Today was one of those days.

And yet something is different.

I know what to do.

I plunge into cold water and let the body recalibrate.

I walk with my dog and feel my feet strike the ground.

I choose presence instead of projection.

I move toward meaning instead of relief.

The agitation passes.

Not because I am cured.

Because I am oriented.

Five months ago, dysregulation would have carried me.

Now it visits and leaves.

I am not healed.

But I am not the same man who sat on that deck in May staring at gray.

The difference is not perfection.

It is hierarchy.

Ego no longer running unchecked.

Shadow no longer acting alone.

Faith no longer sentimental.

I have structure now.

And structure changes everything.

The work is not finished.

It has begun.

Chapter Ten

STRUCTURE AND THE SEVEN PILLARS

I want to tell you something about those first 120 days that I couldn't see while I was inside them.

I wasn't white-knuckling my way through recovery on willpower and conviction. I know that's what it can look like from the outside — a man making a decision and holding it. But that's not what was actually happening. Willpower was never going to be enough. I had tried willpower. I had tried conviction. I had tried the sheer force of not wanting to be this man anymore. None of it held. Not once, across years of attempts.

What held this time was different. It was structural.

The Tenets kept my aperture and perspective constructively open during recovery. What I came to realize that something else was holding me structurally — seven things operating underneath everything.

The siege, the gray corridor, New Zealand, the return home — I can see now what I couldn't see then. Seven things were operating underneath everything else. Not as a program I was following. As infrastructure I was slowly, sometimes unconsciously, bringing back online. When they were all running together, I held. When one went dark, I felt the edges soften within hours.

I'm going to name them now because I think they're worth naming. Not as a prescription. As an accounting of what actually kept me upright.

You've already watched them work. This is just the map of what you witnessed.

Spiritual Alignment

For most of those ninety days, the first thing I did every morning was read Scripture. Not snippets- but chapter... books. The long ones with blood and consequence and a God who doesn't behave the way you'd expect.

I didn't do this because I felt spiritual. Most mornings I didn't. I did it because I had learned, through enough failed attempts at recovery, that the first input of the day sets the governing authority for everything that follows. When God was first, something in my nervous system had a vertical reference point before the world got its hands on me. When the phone was first — the news, the scroll, the ambient noise of a dopamine economy that had learned exactly how to capture my attention before I was fully awake — the day belonged to something else by the time I was vertical.

The days I skipped it I could feel the loosening by midmorning. Not guilt. Something more mechanical than guilt. The internal governor going quiet. Impulse moving into the space that conscience had vacated.

What I found when I actually went looking — was a God who wrestles. Who grieves. Who delivers and judges and restores. A Jesus who wasn't a metaphysical symbol but a man, a suffering man, who stood in front of corrupted power with a quietness that shook empires and died at the hands of the same weak, threatened egomaniacs who still populate the earth.

That God I could actually talk to.

I started.

Slowly. Inconsistently.

Genesis. Luke. Jeremiah. Ezekiel.

The long ones. The painful ones.

I now met God without the metaphysics.

Not a symbol.

Not a principle.

Not a sanitized abstraction.

A God who wrestles.

A God who grieves.

A God who burns.

A God who delivers.

A God who judges.

A God who restores.

A God who is terrifyingly real and inexplicably tender.

I stopped seeing faith as a dopamine hit, an emotional high, a fix.

I stopped confusing spiritual feeling with spiritual reality.

Something in me shifted.

My love for God matured.

My prayers matured.

The fog began to thin.

I used to pray the way a desperate man bargains — promises, tears, vows I couldn't keep. I would fall to my knees trying to outrun the consequences of my own choices. It never worked. It wasn't prayer. It was panic.

Now my prayers aren't chemical dumps.

They aren't frantic deals.

They aren't self-centered.

They are simple, grounded, sober:

For my family.

For my sons.

For people I love who cannot love me back.

For people drowning in the same compulsions I escaped.

For strangers who need a foothold.

For the broken.

For the world.

For clarity.

For alignment.

For strength.

For obedience.

For God's will — not mine.

Fuel

I had spent most of my consulting years running on adrenaline dressed up as discipline. Breakfast was whatever I grabbed between the hotel room (often-times a Coke and a Snickers bar) and the first meeting. Sometimes nothing. I thought I was operating at a high level. I was operating on a depleted system that had learned to mask depletion with cortisol, and I was paying a tab I couldn't see accumulating.

What I understand now is that hunger is one of the most reliable triggers in existence- because a hungry brain is a brain in mild crisis, and a brain in mild crisis reaches for whatever has historically made the crisis stop fastest. For me that was never food. The compulsive loop existed to solve the same problem a real breakfast could have solved, and I had been letting it do that job for decades.

The foodie in me is dead. It cost my body too much and I don't mourn it.

Food is fuel now. Protein first, every morning, before caffeine touches the system. Whole food. Gluten watched. Sugar watched. Carbs front-loaded, not eaten into the night. Fast food gone. Salty snacks gone. The macros aren't complicated — they just require deciding that your body is worth the attention.

It's not discipline. It's just clarity about what the machine needs to run.

Things were changing at a level below what I could consciously track. The fuel system coming online was part of how I knew.

The Body

When a nervous system has been running in threat mode for decades, stress chemistry accumulates in the body the way pressure accumulates in a sealed pipe. It has to go somewhere- mine usually went into compulsion. Into alcohol. Into the controlled aggression that consulting rewards and that everything else in a man's life eventually cannot survive. Once those outlets were closed, I needed somewhere else to put it or it was going to find its own exit.

Training became that exit. Not as a discipline practice. As pressure management. The cold plunge not as a biohack but as the only thing that reliably brought my nervous system down from the ceiling on the days when nothing else could reach it. The sauna as regulation, not luxury. Walking as the simplest available way to move the chemistry of a hard day out of my body before it became the chemistry of a bad decision. Upper body 2X per week. Legs 2X per week. Keep the routine... but any movement is better than no movement.

I didn't understand all of this mechanically while it was happening. I understood it the way you understand that a window needs to be opened when a room has gone stale. The body knew before the mind caught up.

Nervous System Regulation

This is the one everything else turns on.

The prefrontal cortex is where judgment lives. Where restraint lives. Where the version of you that knows better actually has the leverage to act on what he knows. The limbic system is older, faster, and entirely uninterested in your long-term wellbeing. It wants discomfort ended and it wants it ended immediately.

In a regulated nervous system the prefrontal cortex governs. The limbic system has a voice but not a veto.

Mine had been inverted for years. The limbic system ran the show and the prefrontal cortex sat somewhere behind glass — watching, generating insight, producing the internal narration of a man who knew exactly what he was doing wrong and could not stop doing it. This is why intelligent men do things they cannot explain afterward. It is not stupidity. It is not weakness. It is a nervous system that has been trained, through years of high-intensity stimulation, to hand control to the wrong part of the brain.

The hierarchy doesn't reverse through insight alone. It reverses through the accumulated effect of the other pillars — through sleep returning, through physical discharge, through removing the chemical inputs that were keeping the limbic system artificially elevated. Over weeks the pause between trigger and action lengthens. Then lengthens again.

Somewhere around week three an ordinary afternoon produced a trigger and I watched it move through me without taking me anywhere. The craving rose, registered, and passed. I stayed where I was.

This was new territory for me. I didn't know until that moment that it was possible.

Psychological Integration

There is the version of yourself you show the world. And there is the rest of you.

The version I showed the world was competent, direct, high-functioning — the man who could walk into any level of organizational chaos and find the load-bearing problem within hours. That version was real. It was also partial. What it didn't show — what it actively suppressed — was the hunger underneath. The loneliness. The grief that never metabolized. The rage at powerlessness that I had learned very early was not safe to express. All of it went underground.

What nobody tells you is that what you bury doesn't disappear. It goes into the basement and it lifts weights down there. And eventually it comes up through the floorboards — as compulsion, as rage disproportionate to whatever small thing triggered it, as the behavior at 3 a.m. that contradicts everything the daytime version of you believes about himself.

My therapist walked me into this territory at a pace my nervous system could handle. She didn't need the story to be clean. She saw the patterns before I named them and she helped me understand what had happened to me as a child — the boundary violations, the psychological warfare that looked invisible from the outside and felt corrosive from the inside — as injury rather than identity.

Denial is expensive. It keeps you loyal to the wrong explanation for why you are the way you are. And as long as you have the wrong explanation, you keep applying the wrong solution.

The gap between who I was in daylight and who I became after dark has closed. That gap — the fracture between the persona and the shadow — is where compulsion lives. When it closes, the compulsion loses its address.

Neuroscience

I spent years believing my compulsive behavior was a moral problem. A character defect. Something broken in me at the level of identity. That framing kept me locked in shame, and shame is the most effective way to ensure a man never actually changes — because it tells him the problem is what he is rather than what his nervous system learned to do.

Week one of understanding the actual science ended that.

Dopamine is not the pleasure chemical. It is the anticipation chemical. It fires not when you get the thing but when you expect the thing. The compulsive loop was never about desire. It was about a brain trained through thousands of repetitions to spike on the anticipation of relief — and to treat that spike as non-negotiable. The behavior wasn't the addiction. The anticipation was.

Once I understood that I stopped trying to fight desire and started interrupting pattern. Those are entirely different problems with entirely different solutions. You cannot white-knuckle your way out of a dopamine loop for the same reason you cannot decide your way out of a fever. But you can understand the loop well enough to stop feeding it. And you can build the regulatory infrastructure that lets the brain slowly rewire itself over weeks and months.

Understanding the mechanism didn't fix anything by itself. But it ended the shame spiral that had been keeping me from fixing anything. I wasn't defective. I was a human nervous system that had been handed inputs it was never designed to process at the volume and intensity the modern world delivers them. That is not an excuse. It is a starting point. A man who understands his own machinery can actually work on it. A man drowning in shame about his machinery just keeps drowning.

Boundary Setting

Boundaries are not what I demand from other people.

I thought a boundary was a line I drew around myself and defended against intrusion. That's not a boundary. That's a fortification. Fortifications require constant energy to maintain and they keep out everything — threatening and nourishing alike.

A real boundary is an expression of who you are. It is the distance between your values and your behavior closing. It is a decision made in advance about what you will and will not participate in.

I had no trouble holding external boundaries. Telling a hostile client or a dishonest partner where the line was — that I could do without hesitation, because it lived in the professional world where I had decades of competence and confidence to draw on.

The internal ones were gone. Had been gone so long I'd stopped registering the absence. The boundary between what I said I valued and what I actually did. Between the man I was at my sons' events and the man I was alone at midnight. Between the life I was performing and the life I was actually living.

Rebuilding those boundaries didn't feel like setting rules. It felt like becoming someone who no longer needed to negotiate with himself about certain things. Hard stops on the digital architecture of the loop. Hard stops on the environments and inputs that had been feeding it for years. Not imposed from outside — arising from a self that was finally clear enough to make them and mean them.

There is a boundary held by willpower — exhausting, constantly renegotiated, one bad day away from collapse. And there is a boundary held by identity. The second one doesn't feel like restraint. It feels like who you are.

I'm not fully at the second one yet. But I know what it feels like now because I've felt it hold under pressure that would have taken me apart a year ago.

The System

None of these seven things work in isolation. I know because I tried them that way for years.

A cleaner diet for a month. A commitment to sobriety for six weeks. Exercise for a season. Bible reading until it felt routine and I stopped. Each one real, each one insufficient, because a system doesn't stabilize when you fix one part and leave the others dark. The pressure finds the weakness and comes through there. Every time.

What those first ninety days taught me — what I can see clearly now that I couldn't see while I was inside it — is that these seven things are interdependent in a way that makes partial effort almost pointless. Energy affects mood. Mood affects impulse. Impulse determines whether a boundary holds. A broken boundary produces shame. Shame degrades sleep. Degraded sleep tanks metabolic stability. Unstable metabolism destabilizes the nervous system. A dysregulated nervous system makes spiritual contact feel hollow and psychological integration collapse under the pressure of the next trigger.

The whole thing runs together or it doesn't run.

When all seven came online simultaneously something shifted that willpower alone had never been able to touch. Not dramatically. The dread that had greeted every morning of my adult life simply... stopped. I woke up and my body was asking for breakfast. Centered. Rested. Hungry.

I didn't understand in that moment exactly what had changed or why. I only knew that something had.

Now I know what it was.

It was the system coming back online.

Chapter Eleven

FOUNDATION

After all this, I do not feel dramatically different inside.

I don't wake up feeling like a transformed man. My companies are not suddenly surging. My inbox is not overflowing with opportunity. My external life would not impress anyone looking for visible proof. Some parts of it feel transitional. Some parts feel unresolved. Nothing announces victory.

And yet something fundamental has shifted.

I no longer cope in the extremes. I no longer detonate when challenged or spiral when disappointed. I no longer anesthetize boredom with stimulation. I no longer allow a single conversation or a single outcome to define my worth. The volatility that once governed my interior life has quieted.

If I once had a dollar of attention to spend each day, half of it went to outrage, sexual compulsivity, comparison, procrastination, and restless mental noise. That half-dollar is no longer lost. It has been reclaimed. It now moves toward work that matters, toward writing that clarifies, toward conversations that are deliberate rather than reactive. It moves toward presence.

I have learned that attention is not infinite. Where it goes, identity follows.

My mornings are anchored now. Scripture before headlines. Cold water before email. Protein before caffeine spikes. Movement before argument. Silence before noise. These are not rituals of fragility. They are disciplines of orientation. Without structure, I drift into old grooves. With structure, I remain steady.

There are still days when agitation rises. There are still mornings when uncertainty presses on me. There are still moments when I feel the old reflex scanning for validation, for urgency, for proof that I matter. The difference is that those reflexes no longer run unchecked. I notice them. I regulate. I choose.

I listen more carefully now. I interrupt less. I feel less need to win the room. I no longer posture intellectually to secure space. I am slower to react and quicker to reflect. I do not chase intensity to feel alive. I do not need to manufacture friction to feel engaged.

Five months ago, my interior felt like a constant negotiation between persona and impulse. I was either performing strength or managing shame. Now there is less internal argument. Less bargaining. Less hidden tension.

I am not healed in the cinematic sense. I am not perfected. I am not beyond temptation or doubt.

But I am less divided.

And being less divided changes everything.

My Act III has not yet been written. There is no dramatic reveal waiting at the end of this chapter. But the foundation has been laid. I know how to keep my nervous system ordered. I know how to interrupt loops before they take hold. I know how to metabolize discomfort instead of escaping it. I know how to sit in stillness without reaching for noise.

That is new.

There was a time when vigilance ran my life. When performance was protection. When urgency felt like oxygen. That part of me was not evil.

It was adaptive. It kept me functioning in environments that demanded armor.

I do not despise that part of me.

I speak to it differently now.

And then there are the dishes.

I run the water into the right side of the sink until it's hot. A few drops of soap. Fill the left side for rinsing. I organize what goes into the dishwasher and what gets washed by hand. Then I work through the hand-wash items smallest to largest — knives and spatulas before the pots and pans.

I like the feeling of the hot soapy water. I like the organization of it. I like the moment when the last pan is rinsed and dried and put away and the sink is clean and the counter is clear.

I like improving the process every time I do it.

Two years ago this was not my job. I would have used it as evidence of something — imbalance, disrespect, the accumulation of small grievances I was always keeping score of. I would have done it badly or not at all, and either way it would have cost something. A tone. A comment. A door closed harder than it needed to be.

Now I just wash the dishes.

Not because I have to.

Not because someone is watching.

Not because it proves anything about who I am or earns me anything in return.

Because it is mine to do. Because the water is hot. Because the process is satisfying. Because I am standing in my kitchen at the end of an ordinary day and I am present inside it in a way I was not capable of being two years ago.

This is what the other side of all of it looks like.

Just a man. A sink. Hot water. The smallest things washed first.

Present.

Enough.

ACKNOWLEDGEMENTS

To my beloved sons. You know the truth. It ends with you… and it begins with you.

To my therapist. Thank you for the care you showed in helping me face my shadow—and, most importantly, for being someone I could trust.

To the authors, thinkers, and voices whose work shaped my understanding and influenced this journey:

- Marcus Aurelius
- Viktor Frankl
- Gabor Maté
- Carl Jung
- James Hollis
- Edward Edinger
- Bessel van der Kolk
- Laurence Heller
- Mary Karr
- Eben Alexander

Your work helped illuminate a path that once felt impossible to see.

THE SEVEN PILLARS FRAMEWORK

There is a point in collapse where motivation no longer works.

Not because a person is weak — but because the system they are living inside has become incoherent.

And no amount of insight could compensate for a disordered internal system.

The Seven Pillars are the structural systems that bring a human organism back online — biologically, psychologically, morally, and relationally.

Each pillar governs a different subsystem.

Each one must be restored for the whole system to function.

You don't "try" these.

You **rebuild them.**

And once they are online, recovery stops feeling like a fight — and starts functioning like a system again.

1. SPIRITUAL ALIGNMENT

Subsystem Governed: Meaning, conscience, impulse restraint, moral gravity

a. What This Pillar Is

Spiritual alignment is the act of placing my life under a vertical reference point — not a concept of God, but a living axis of authority higher than appetite, fear, and self-interest.

This is the system that governs conscience.

Without it, impulse becomes king.

b. What Breaks When It Fails

When this pillar is offline:

- Meaning collapses into mood
- Desire outranks conviction
- Comfort outranks character
- Self-justification replaces self-restraint

The psyche becomes horizontally organized around relief, approval, and stimulation.

The organism becomes **dopamine-led instead of conscience-led.**

This is not a moral failure.

It is a *systems failure.*

c. Failure State

Failure is not "sin." Failure is **loss of vertical reference.**

It begins with skipping first contact.

When the day opens without God as the highest authority, the nervous system immediately defaults to threat-relief scanning:

Scrolling.

Numbing.

Soothing.

Avoiding.

Rationalizing.

Once impulse is installed as governor, every choice afterward is compromised.

Shame and guilt appear because conscious behavior is now misaligned with subconscious values — creating internal incoherence, stress chemistry, and vulnerability to relapse.

d. What Alignment Restores

When this pillar is online:

- Conscience regains authority
- Impulse loses veto power
- Meaning stabilizes mood
- Presence becomes natural
- Energy becomes coherent

Bandwidth returns.

Not motivation.

Bandwidth.

You regain the ability to read, write, create, think, and act without friction because your nervous system is no longer negotiating with appetite.

Alignment restores **internal governance.**

e. The Anchor

My daily anchor is immediate vertical contact.

Before image, input, or obligation — I place my nervous system under God's authority.

Scripture.

Contemplation.

Integration.

I turn understanding into personal command structure for the day.

This is not devotional — it is *regulatory.*

f. The Cost of Failure

One image.

One scroll.

One ungoverned input can reinstall impulse as governor.

Once that happens:

- Nervous system volatility increases
- Presence must be forced
- Triggers must be actively suppressed
- Recovery tax begins

It can take up to two days to restore full coherence.

This is not punishment.

This is **neurobiological consequence.**

2. FUEL / METABOLIC REGULATION

Subsystem Governed: Cellular energy, cognition, mood stability, inflammation control

a. What This Pillar Is

This pillar governs how the organism produces usable energy.

Food is not stimulation.

Food is metabolic command.

The brain alone consumes roughly 20% of the body's total energy.

When fuel is unstable, *nothing else can stay online.*

Not regulation.

Not clarity.

Not restraint.

Not resilience.

b. What Breaks When It Fails

When metabolic regulation fails:

- Mood destabilizes
- Cognition dulls
- Impulse control weakens
- Inflammation rises
- Nervous system regulation becomes fragile
- Physical training stops producing adaptive signal

The organism becomes chemically underpowered.

This is not a willpower problem.

It is an **energy crisis.**

c. Failure State

Failure expresses as:

- Hunger-driven emotional volatility
- Brain fog
- Systemic inflammation
- Gut permeability
- Dopamine-seeking feeding behavior

Hunger becomes one of the most powerful relapse triggers because the body begins demanding *relief*, not nourishment.

d. What Alignment Restores

When aligned:

- Protein availability stabilizes muscle and hormones
- Carbohydrate availability supports cognition
- Gut-derived serotonin stabilizes mood
- Inflammation drops
- Energy becomes even and predictable

The organism stops swinging between depletion and stimulation.

e. The Anchor

My daily anchor is non-negotiable metabolic stability.

A protein-forward breakfast reinstalls chemical balance before the day begins.

This replaced years of vending-machine sugar, caffeine, and depletion.

This is not preference — it is physiological governance.

f. The Cost of Failure

Failure produces:

- Irritability
- Confusion
- Weakness
- Joint, gut, and facial inflammation
- Fatigue
- Trigger susceptibility
- Mood instability

Once the fuel system destabilizes, everything else becomes harder.

3. BODY / STRENGTH & RESILIENCE

Subsystem Governed: Hormonal signaling, physical confidence, stress discharge, survivability, recovery capacity

a. What This Pillar Is

This pillar governs whether the body is structurally capable.

Strength training, cardiovascular conditioning, and calisthenics are not "exercise." They are **hormonal and neurological commands.**

Movement instructs the endocrine system how to allocate testosterone, growth hormone, dopamine, endorphins, insulin sensitivity, and mitochondrial output.

A strong body does not just look better.

It **regulates chemistry, stress, and confidence.**

b. What Breaks When It Fails

When this subsystem goes offline:

- Confidence collapses
- Posture degrades
- Mobility narrows
- Injury risk rises
- Insulin sensitivity drops
- Stress accumulates without discharge
- Body composition deteriorates
- Longevity trajectory steepens downward

The organism becomes fragile.

c. Failure State

Failure is not "being out of shape." Failure is **lack of mechanical load.**

The system loses:

- Oxygenation
- Muscular signaling
- Metabolic throughput
- Stress discharge pathways

Which produces:

- Atrophy
- Weakness
- Insulin resistance
- Chronic fatigue
- Bottled internal pressure — with no safe outlet

d. What Alignment Restores

When aligned:

- Energy is discharged instead of suppressed
- Muscle mass increases survivability and lifespan
- Flexibility improves recovery and reduces injury
- Posture stabilizes breathing and authority
- Hormones normalize
- Cognition sharpens
- The body becomes a stable platform instead of a liability

e. The Anchor

My training rhythm:

- Upper body — twice weekly
- Legs and core — twice weekly
- Walking or cycling on off days

Movement is not optional.

It is a **primary regulation tool.**

Under trigger load, calisthenics are used immediately to interrupt compulsive loops by physically discharging stress chemistry.

4. NERVOUS SYSTEM REGULATION

Subsystem Governed: Threat processing, impulse control, baseline safety, sleep, libido, emotional stability

a. What This Pillar Is

This pillar governs **who is in charge inside the nervous system.**

The limbic system exists to detect threat and drive survival reflexes.

The prefrontal cortex exists to govern meaning, restraint, foresight, and choice.

Regulation means these systems perform their intended roles — instead of reversing authority.

b. What Breaks When It Fails

When regulation fails, chronic dopamine stimulation rewires the reward system.

New circuitry forms around relief-seeking, bypassing prefrontal screening.

Impulse becomes governor.

Threat and appetite run the system.

The organism loses the ability to pause, evaluate, and choose.

This is not lack of discipline — it is **neurological hijack.**

c. Failure State

Failure expresses as compulsive loops:

Trigger → Ritual → Relief → Crash → Repeat

Which produces:

- Addiction
- Time and money hemorrhage
- Purpose erosion
- Relationship collapse
- Reputation damage
- Employment instability
- Guilt, shame, depression

- Forward momentum stall

The system becomes self-consuming.

d. What Alignment Restores

When aligned:

- Prefrontal governance returns
- Triggers lose authority
- Neuroplasticity begins reversing hijack pathways
- Presence returns
- Capacity expands
- Peace stabilizes

The organism regains internal leadership.

e. The Anchor

This pillar is supported by every other pillar.

Regulation is the hinge.

The prefrontal cortex must come back online and re-assume command.

This is the difference between surviving and governing your life.

5. PSYCHOLOGICAL INTEGRATION

Subsystem Governed: Ego, shadow, Self, identity coherence, trigger processing, individuation

a. What This Pillar Is

This pillar governs **who you are being — not what you are doing.**

Psychological integration is the alignment of ego, subconscious, and Self into a coherent operating system.

It is the condition in which:

- Your values are internalized
- Your reactions are conscious
- Your identity is stable
- Your behavior is congruent

It is the difference between *living your life* and *performing your life.*

b. What Breaks When It Fails

When this pillar goes offline, ego inflation replaces integration.

The psyche compensates with:

- Performance
- Manipulation
- Compulsion
- Image management
- False attachment
- Hubris

Value becomes externalized.

Worth becomes comparative.

Purpose dissolves.

The addictive loop is fed because the Self is no longer governing the system.

c. Failure State

Failure is loss of trigger awareness and emotional sovereignty.

The limbic brain will fabricate narratives — fantasy, grievance, unresolved trauma — to reinstall old coping loops.

A slip is not collapse.

Collapse is sustained limbic governance.

Failure looks like:

- Using unhealthy coping to avoid pain or discomfort
- Trading presence for relief

d. What Alignment Restores

When aligned:

- Regulation stabilizes
- Clarity returns
- Presence deepens
- Empathy softens perception
- Communication becomes natural
- Flow becomes default

Your internal filter clears.

You re-enter the world without compulsive distortion.

Life becomes vivid again — color, texture, grief, joy — without the need to manage, perform, or escape.

This is not emotionalism.

This is **individuation.**

e. The Anchor

My anchor is ego governance.

Triggers are recognized early.

Pain is allowed to pass through without reaction.

The ego becomes an efficient operating system — not a defense mechanism.

Sit with your pain.

It is trying to teach you something.

6. NEUROSCIENCE APPLICATION

Subsystem Governed: Dopamine circuitry, cortisol/adrenaline balance, threat normalization, impulse screening, sleep–wake stability

a. What This Pillar Is

This pillar governs **mechanism awareness and intervention.**

Neuroscience application is the conscious understanding of how trauma, guilt, shame, and false value imprinting alter the brain's reward and threat systems.

Repeated reliance on fast dopamine creates new circuitry that bypasses prefrontal screening and hands control to the limbic system.

Impulse becomes automatic.

Relief becomes compulsory.

Choice becomes compromised.

This is not moral failure.

This is **neuroplastic adaptation.**

b. What Breaks When It Fails

When this pillar is offline:

- Tolerance escalates — novelty must increase
- Rational decision making degrades

- Risk tolerance rises
- Fight-or-flight becomes dysregulated
- Cortisol, adrenaline, and dopamine flood the system
- Sleep fragments
- Inflammation increases
- Digestion, cognition, and joint function suffer

The body becomes chemically volatile.

c. Failure State

Failure is **mechanism blindness.**

Ignoring the rules of the nervous system guarantees predictable collapse.

Failure looks like:

- Escalating novelty and danger
- Relationship instability
- Emotional volatility
- Depression
- Financial and employment damage
- Boundary erosion

The system eats itself.

d. What Alignment Restores

When aligned:

- Prefrontal governance returns
- Mood chemistry stabilizes
- Risk appetite normalizes
- Sleep and appetite regulate
- Choice becomes available again

You regain authorship of your behavior.

e. The Anchor

My anchor is mechanism awareness.

I understand what compulsive behavior does to my chemistry — and I intervene early.

I am not broken.

I am not evil.

I am not defective.

I am human biology responding to imprint and environment.

And with understanding comes sovereignty.

7. BOUNDARY SETTING

Subsystem Governed: Emotional sovereignty, relational safety, integrity, agency, attachment security

a. What This Pillar Is

This pillar governs **who has access to you — and on what terms.**

Boundaries are not walls.

They are **sovereign perimeter control.**

Healthy relationship dynamics are not about managing other people.

They are about governing your own actions, values, reactions, and availability.

You do not control others.

You control your access, your consent, your behavior, and your integrity.

b. What Breaks When It Fails

When this pillar goes offline:

- Sovereignty is traded for approval
- Dignity is traded for influence
- Agency is traded for chemical echoes
- Reality is traded for fantasy
- Emotional safety erodes
- Attachment becomes transactional

The system becomes externally governed.

c. Failure State

Failure is loss of internal value anchoring.

Value is no longer received — it is chased.

Failure expresses as:

- Enmeshment
- Validation-seeking
- Manipulation
- Compulsive monitoring of messages *(hypervigilant attachment scanning)*
- Faux intimacy
- Flattery replacing connection

You begin negotiating your identity through others.

d. What Alignment Restores

When aligned:

- Integrity replaces narrative management

- Truth replaces illusion
- Depth replaces speed
- Reality replaces fantasy
- Vulnerability restores safety
- Trust stabilizes attachment
- Real love replaces performative connection

You become safe — and selective.

e. The Anchor

My daily anchor is value anchoring.

My worth does not come from admiration, performance, income, or influence.

It is received — and honored — not extracted.

My thoughts, posture, speech, and behavior express that truth.

Boundaries are not what I demand from others.

They are what I **embody.**

They determine who can walk with me — and who cannot.

The Integration Bridge

Before any of these pillars become habits, they must become **infrastructure.**

A human being is not a collection of behaviors.

A human being is an integrated system.

Energy affects mood.

Mood affects impulse.

Impulse affects boundaries.

Boundaries affect relationships.

Relationships affect nervous system safety.

Safety affects sleep.

Sleep affects judgment.

Judgment affects everything.

This is why partial recovery fails.

You cannot stabilize the nervous system while starving the body.

You cannot heal impulse while your meaning structure is collapsed.

You cannot integrate psychologically while your chemistry is volatile.

The pillars are not additive.

They are **interdependent.**

You do not "do" them.

You **bring them online.**

And once they are online, recovery stops feeling like a fight — and starts functioning like a system again.

ABOUT THE AUTHOR

Tony Crandall is a finance executive and advisor with more than thirty years of experience helping organizations navigate complex operational and financial transformation. Over the course of his career, he has worked with global consulting firms including PwC, IBM, and EY, leading large-scale initiatives in finance, systems implementation, and organizational performance.

Behind that professional life ran a quieter, more difficult story—one shaped by early trauma, relentless performance pressure, and the slow erosion that can occur when a life is built on survival rather than integration.

Rewired Restored emerged from the work that followed.

Through a rigorous process of personal reconstruction—spanning neuroscience, psychology, philosophy, and spiritual inquiry—Tony began rebuilding the internal systems that govern human stability: nervous system regulation, identity coherence, metabolic health, moral alignment, and relational integrity.

Today he writes and speaks about the intersection of nervous system regulation, trauma recovery, the modern dopamine economy, and the process of psychological and spiritual integration. His work focuses on helping others understand how high-functioning lives can mask internal fragmentation—and how recovery becomes possible when the underlying systems are rebuilt.

Tony lives in Ohio and continues to explore the relationship between resilience, meaning, and human flourishing. When he is not writing or advising clients, he can often be found traveling, riding motorcycles, bird-watching, playing frisbee with his dog, reading deeply, or spending time with his sons.

www.ingramcontent.com/pod-product-compliance
Lightning Source LLC
LaVergne TN
LVHW010704110826
845149LV00014B/3224